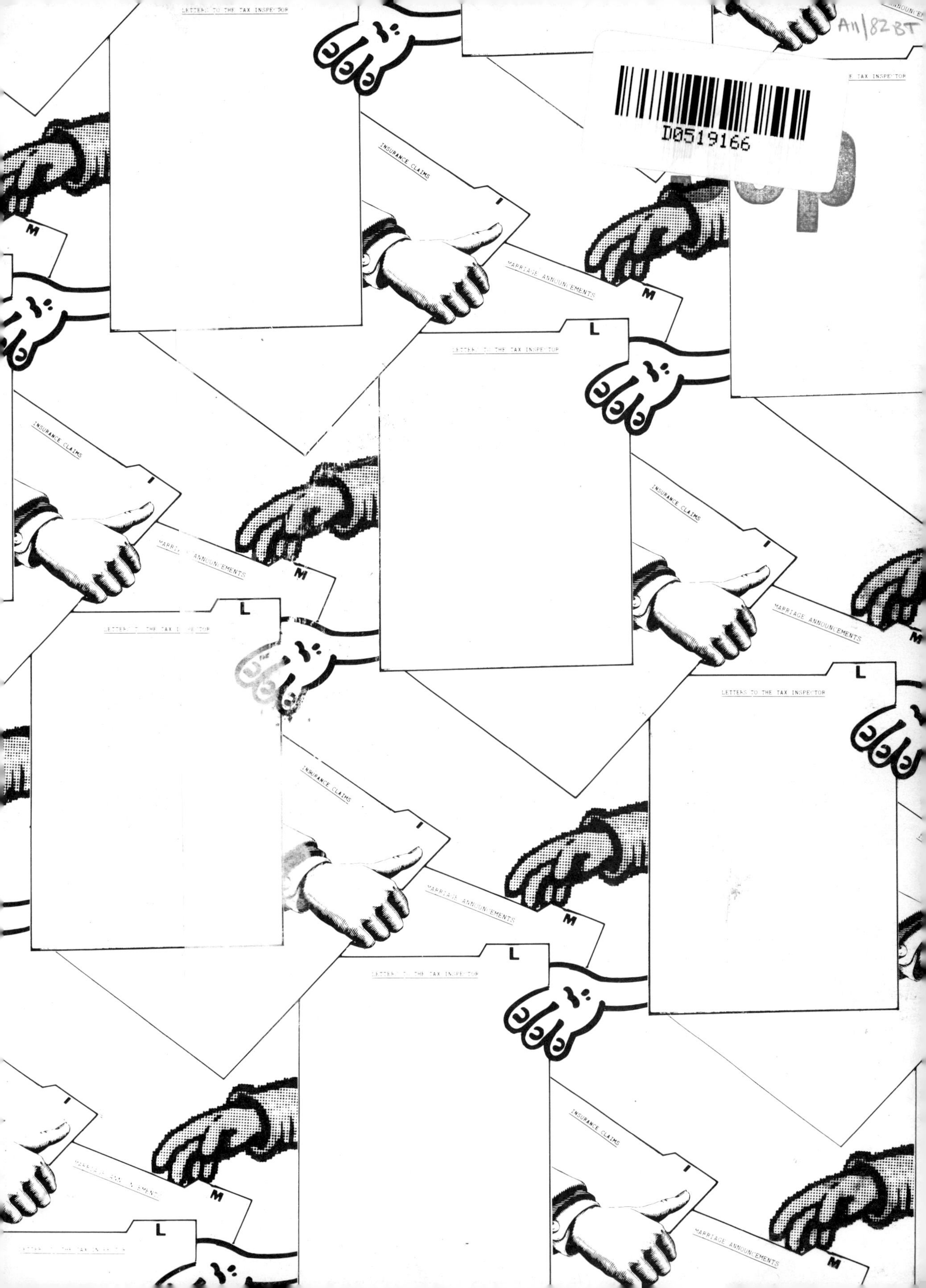
LETTERS TO THE TAX INSPECTOR
INSURANCE CLAIMS
MARRIAGE ANNOUNCEMENTS
L
I
M
D0519166

JOHN DUNN'S
Curious COLLECTION

KIRKCALDY DISTRICT LIBRARIES
386235
827 DUN
BT

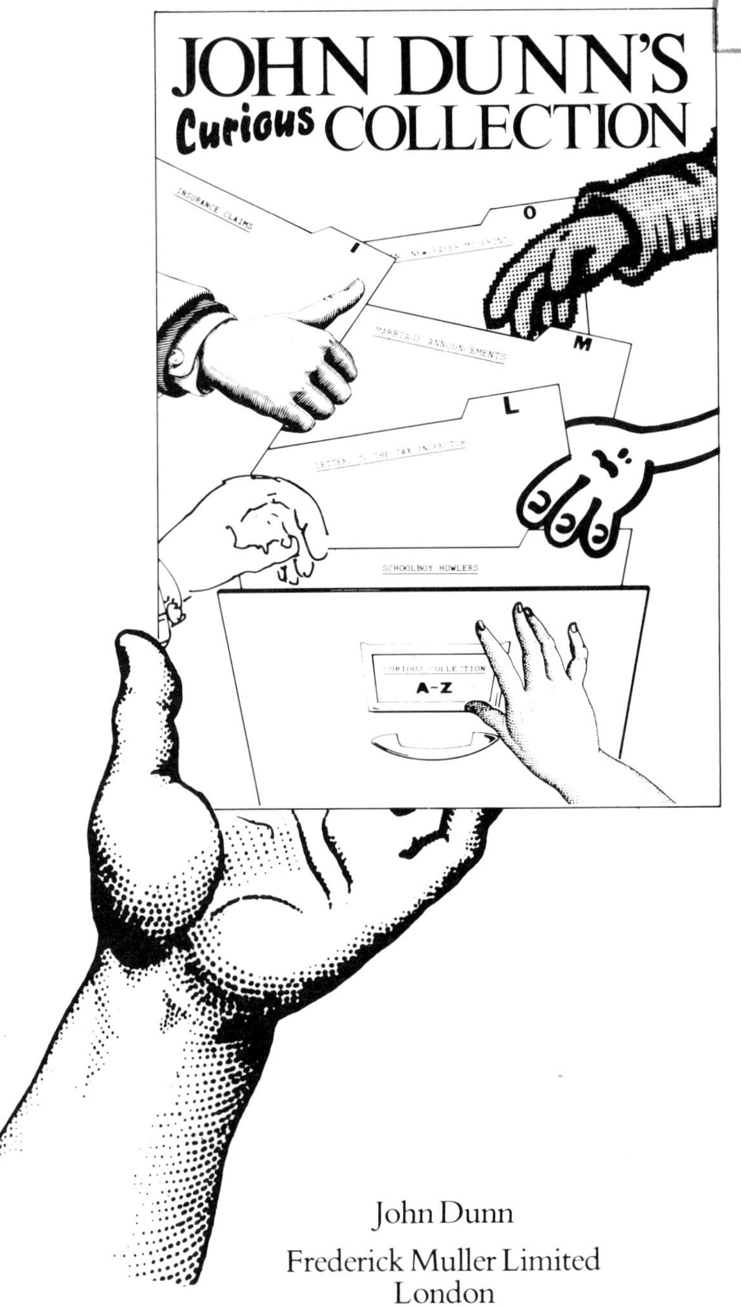

John Dunn

Frederick Muller Limited
London

First published in Great Britain in 1982 by
Frederick Muller Limited, Dataday House,
London SW19 7JL

Copyright © John Dunn and Lennard Books 1982

All rights reserved. No part of this
publication may be reproduced, stored in
a retrieval system, or transmitted, in any
form or by any means, electronic, mechanical,
photocopying, recording or otherwise, without
the prior consent of Frederick Muller Ltd

ISBN 0 584 95030 6

Made by Lennard Books
The Old School
Wheathampstead
Herts AL4 8AN

Editor Michael Leitch
Designed by David Pocknell's Company Ltd
Production Reynolds Clark Associates Ltd
Printed and bound in Spain
by TONSA, San Sebastian
Dep. Legal: S. S. 403 - 1982

CONTENTS

Introduction

'Don't touch the back of the wireless set, dear. You'll get an electric shock!' I was always convinced that if I could just open the set at the right moment, there inside would be a tiny Henry Hall's Dance Band playing minute instruments. I mentioned that on the air one day during a programme called *Breakfast Special* and discovered that, far from being alone, half the nation seemed to have had tiny Henry Halls in their sets.

Nor was that all. I soon began to discover that sayings, word games, puzzles, all sorts of things that I thought were peculiar to my family and friends were obviously peculiar to thousands of other people. And so began a collection of what a good friend of mine labelled 'verbal bric-à-brac'.

During the programme I would suggest an idea and the replies would come tumbling out of what I can only describe as a sort of National Attic. And rarely did they come alone. I would get endless lists of excuses offered to insurance companies by errant drivers, all near enough identical – which makes the differences even more interesting. Is this the folk tradition at work?

Who the original authors are is a mystery. Just like those stories that always happened to 'a friend of a friend', there is always a feeling that if we peel back just one more layer we will find the true source. The nearest I came to that concerned the house rules of a small 19th-century mill that made splendid reading – including the request that employees should each bring in a few lumps of coal on cold mornings and that Mr Rogers's permission had to be obtained before trips were made 'to the bottom of the garden'. My father-in-law had carried this dog-eared notice around in his wallet for years, and naturally I fell on it with glee. So that he could have it back I asked a temporary secretary at the BBC to type me a few copies and the following day it appeared in the *Daily Mail*! Thereafter I was kept supplied at regular intervals with the house rules of a small 19th-century mill that made splendid reading. . . . I would like to claim that I had been responsible in part for that gem being released, but on checking back with my father-in-law – guess where he had got it? From a friend of a friend who found it in an old building that was just about to be pulled down.

So the authorship of much of what follows must be in musical terms our old friend 'Trad'. I would like to thank the many, many people who by their kind letters have made the job of presenting radio programmes a source of continuing pleasure. I have tried to avoid too many of the really old chestnuts but some are inevitably present on the theory that even a chestnut is always new to somebody. And finally a very large thank-you to the band of unknown authors because, I still insist, *somebody* must have written the things....

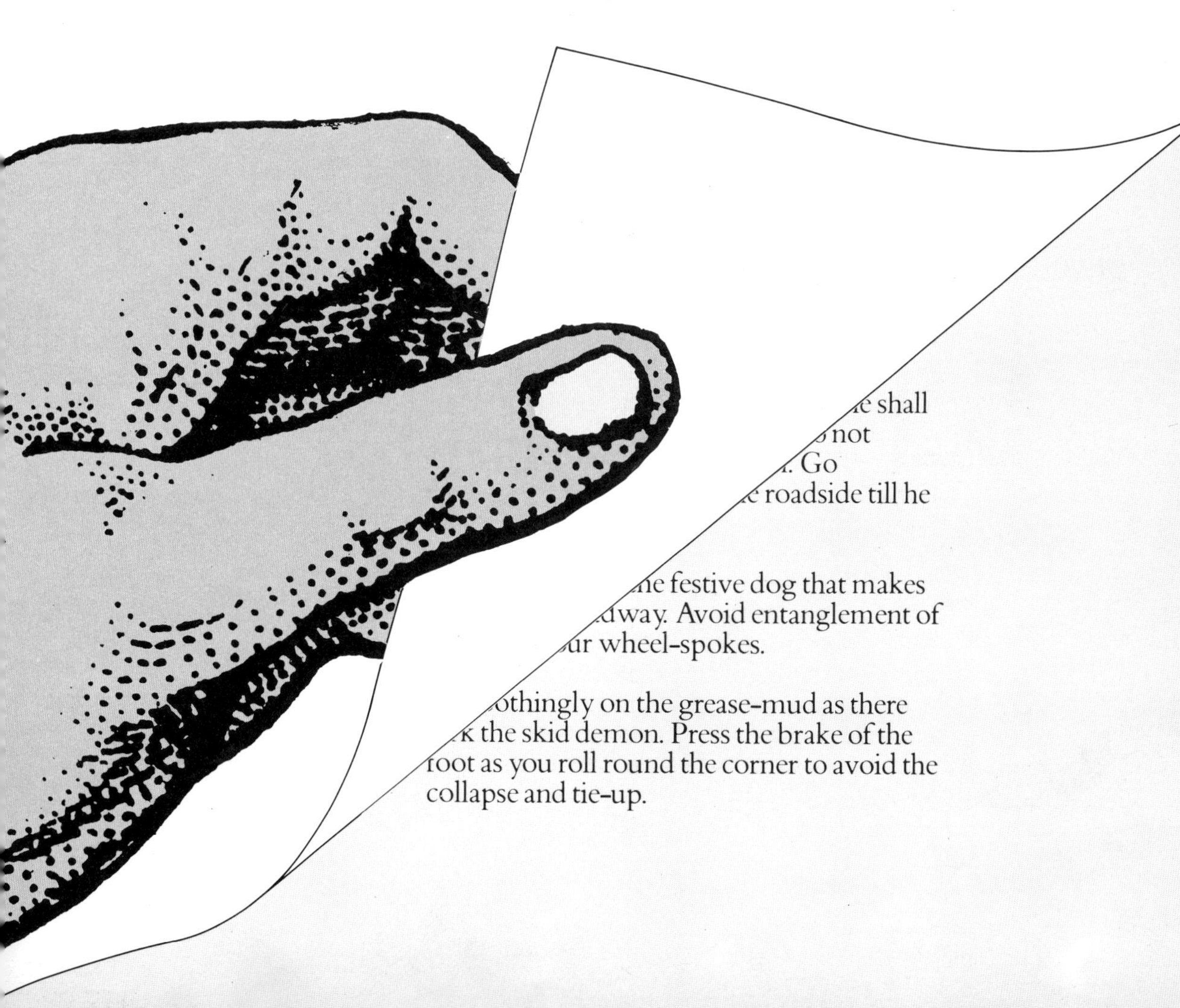

Chapter 1

Beware Of The Wandering Horse

It has been said that no man in a hurry is quite civilized. In which case we started getting very uncivilized in the last years of the 19th century when we began to live with the motor-car. And it hasn't been easy. In America a group called The Farmers Anti-Auto Protection Society proposed some regulations which were intended to ban the snorting beasts that were appearing on the roads in ever-increasing numbers:

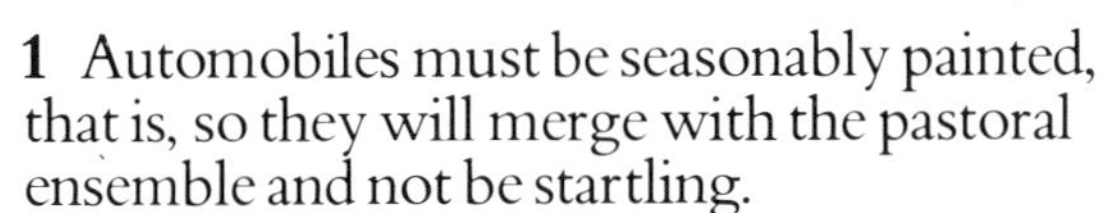

1 Automobiles must be seasonably painted, that is, so they will merge with the pastoral ensemble and not be startling.
2 On discovering an approaching (horse) team, the automobilist must stop off-side and cover his machine with a tarpaulin, painted with the scenery.
3 In case a horse will not pass an automobile, notwithstanding the scenic tarpaulin, the automobilist will take the machine apart as rapidly as possible and conceal the parts in the grass.

4 In case an automobile makes a team run away, the penalty will be 50 dollars for the first mile, 100 dollars for the second, 200 dollars for the third mile, etc, that the team runs, in addition to the usual damages.
5 On approaching a corner where he cannot command a view of the road ahead, the automobilist must stop not less than 100 yards from the turn, toot his horn, ring a bell, fire a revolver, hallo and send up three bombs at intervals of five minutes.
6 Automobiles running on the country roads at night must send up a red rocket every mile and wait 10 minutes for the road to clear. They may then proceed carefully, blowing their horns and shooting their rockets.

Nor was it just the motor car that was viewed with such suspicion. The following notice was to be seen on a railway – need I tell you it was in Ireland – and was reported in the *Cork Constitution* of June 1860:

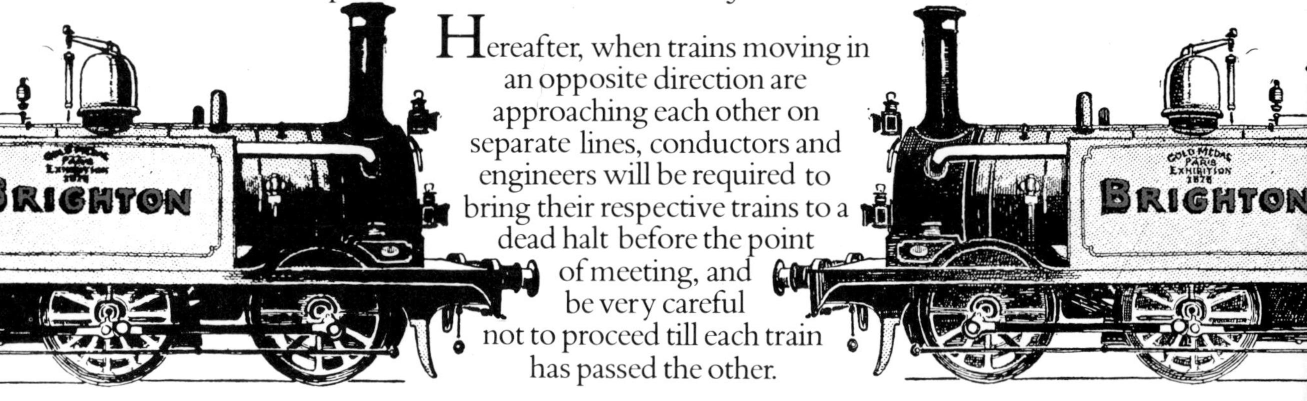

Hereafter, when trains moving in an opposite direction are approaching each other on separate lines, conductors and engineers will be required to bring their respective trains to a dead halt before the point of meeting, and be very careful not to proceed till each train has passed the other.

Official notices, in Britain anyway, never say 'please'; they order, rather than request. So for the nearest thing to charm we have to look abroad. Or perhaps it's just that the early Japanese Rules of the Road gain something in translation:

- At the rise of the hand of policeman, stop rapidly. Do not pass him, or otherwise disrespect him.

- When a passenger of the foot hove in sight, tootle the horn-trumpet to him, melodiously at first. If he still obstacles your passage tootle him with vigour, and express by word of the mouth the warning: 'Hi, Hi!'

- Beware of the wandering horse that he shall not take fright as you pass him. Do not explode the exhaust box at him. Go soothingly by, or stop by the roadside till he pass away.

- Give big space to the festive dog that makes sport in the roadway. Avoid entanglement of dog with your wheel-spokes.

- Go soothingly on the grease-mud as there lurk the skid demon. Press the brake of the foot as you roll round the corner to avoid the collapse and tie-up.

But tying-up was just what the administrators were after. The carefree spirit of those early days had to be shackled. Who, after reading this next edict, could possibly want to be a driver at all?

> The Drivers' Hours (Goods Vehicles) (Keeping of Records) Regulations 1970 S1. 1970 No 123 Regulation 6 (2):
>
> Where an employee-driver changes his employment the employer by whom the employee-driver has ceased to be so employed shall on being so requested by the employee-driver or his new employer, supply the employee-driver or the new employer with such information as is in his possession relating to the whole or any part of a current working week of that employee-driver as is specified in paragraph (4) of this Regulation.

And this comes from the Road Transport Lighting Act of 1967:

> It is hereby declared for the avoidance of doubt that material designed primarily to reflect white light as light of that or another colour is, when reflecting light, to be treated for the purposes of the principal Act as showing a light and material capable of reflecting an image is not, when reflecting the image of a light, to be so treated.

Good. I'm sure that clears up that little point.

The battle between man and motor-car will never be decided. You may think that the car has triumphed already, but consider. You're driving briskly down a clear but wet road, and what happens? An elderly lady waving an orange disc leaps off the pavement. And while your foot is still finding its way to the pedal, let alone seeing if you can stop on the greasy surface, she ushers a dozen smiling children into the road in front of you. It's accidents that bring out the real ingenuity of the motorist. Over the years I have received many 'quotes' from claim forms sent to motor insurance firms. They have two things in common: all are said to be genuine and all are wide-eyed expressions of innocence. Here are a few:

I consider that neither vehicle was to blame but if either were to blame it was the other one.

I knocked over a man. He admitted it was his fault as he had been run over before.

I remember nothing after missing the Crown Hotel until I came to and saw PC Brown.

I collided with a stationary tramcar coming the other way.

I left my Austin Seven outside and when I came out later to my amazement there was an Austin Twelve.

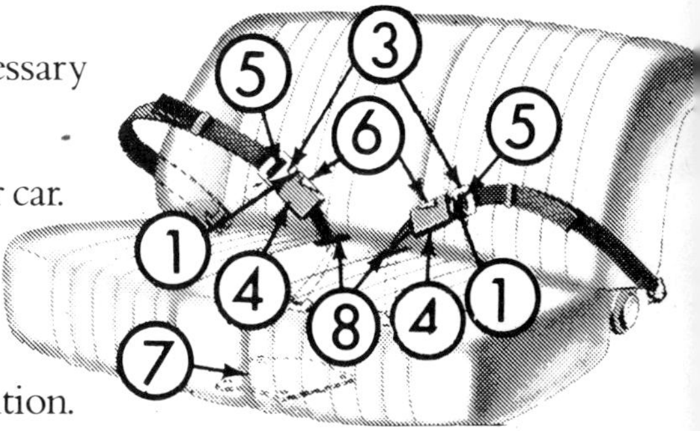

Car had to turn sharper than was necessary owing to an invisible lorry.

To avoid a collision I ran into the other car.

I misjudged a lady crossing the street.

The other car collided with mine without giving any warning of its intention.

The other man altered his mind so I had to run into him.

I told the other idiot what he was and went on.

A pedestrian hit me and went under my car.

I unfortunately ran over a pedestrian and the old gentleman was taken to hospital, much regretting the circumstances.

I thought the side window was down but it was up, as I found when I put my head through it.

If the other driver had stopped a few yards behind himself the accident would not have happened.

She suddenly saw me, lost her head and we met.

Cow wandered into my car. I was afterwards informed that the cow was half-witted.

Three women were talking to each other and when two stepped back and one stepped forward I had to have an accident.

There were plenty of lookers-on but no witnesses.

A bull was standing near and a fly must have tickled him because he gored my car.

I was scraping my nearside on the bank when the accident happened.

After the accident a working gentleman offered to be a witness in my favour.

I collided with a stationary tree.

There was no damage done to the car as the gatepost will testify.

Ice on the road applied brakes causing skid.

One wheel went into the ditch. My foot jumped from brake to accelerator pedal, leapt across the road to the other side and jumped into the trunk of a tree.

The water in my radiator accidentally froze at 12 midnight.

I was taking a friend home and keeping two yards from each lamp post which were in a straight line. Unfortunately, there was a bend in the road bringing the right-hand lamp post in line with the other and of course I landed in a ditch.

I bumped into a lamp post which was obscured by human beings.

I bumped into a shop window and sustained injuries to my wife.

I heard a horn blow and was struck violently in the back. Evidently a lady was trying to pass me.

Coming home I drove into the wrong house and collided with a tree I haven't got.

I can't give details of the accident as I was somewhat concussed at the time.

I blew my horn but it would not work as it was stolen.

A lamp post bumped into my car, damaging it in two places.

My car was stolen and I set up a human cry, but it has not been recovered.

The car in front stopped suddenly and I crashed gently into his luggage grid.

I left my car unattended for a minute, and whether by accident or design it ran away.

I was proceeding along the road at moderate speed when another car rushed out of a side turning and turned upside down in a ditch. It was his fault as he said.

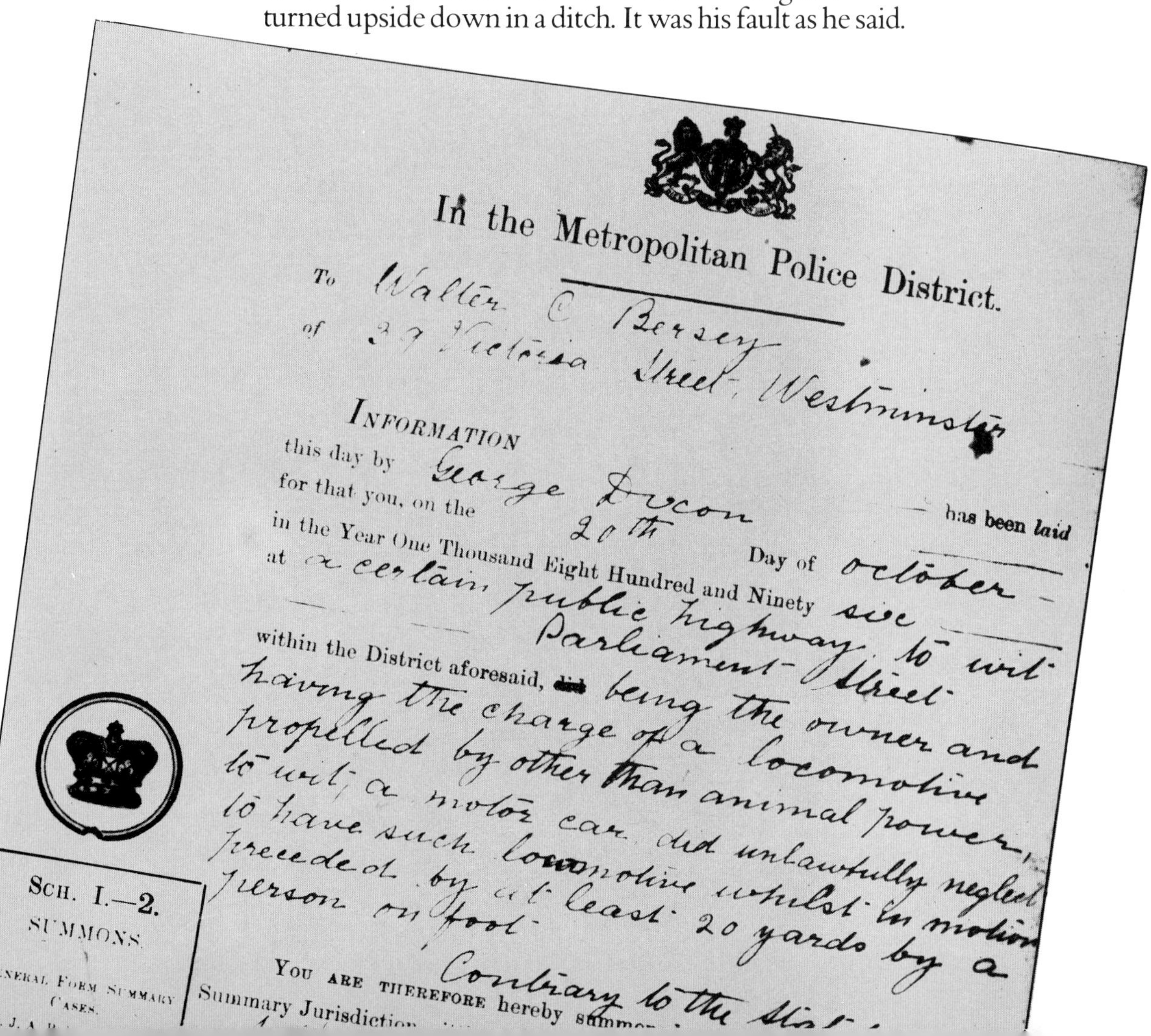

In the Metropolitan Police District.

To Walter C. Bersey

of 39 Victoria Street, Westminster

INFORMATION has been laid this day by George Dixon

for that you, on the 20th Day of October

in the Year One Thousand Eight Hundred and Ninety six

at a certain public highway, to wit Parliament Street

within the District aforesaid, ~~did~~ being the owner and having the charge of a locomotive propelled by other than animal power, to wit, a motor car did unlawfully neglect to have such locomotive whilst in motion preceded by at least 20 yards by a person on foot

Contrary to the Stat...

SCH. I.—2.
SUMMONS.
GENERAL FORM SUMMARY CASES.
S. J. A. ...

YOU ARE THEREFORE hereby summon...
Summary Jurisdiction ...

Chapter 2

Do Not Throw Stones At This Notice

I am almost prepared to swear there was such a notice in a playground of my youth. And certainly it wouldn't have surprised me because the job of adults (and notices) was always to spoil the fun. So I am equally prepared to believe that Newquay has a bye-law that reads:

> No person shall sit, stand, walk, run or lie in these pleasure grounds.
> By Order.

But even if neither of those is true they sound believable because we all know how surrounded we are by petty-minded authority. There is always somebody eager to tell us what to do – although following their instructions may be another matter:

> After you complete an STD call and replace your receiver you are requested to lift the receiver again to hear the dial tone. This is to ensure the receiver is replaced properly.

For some, the great problem with telephones is getting one. A nurse from Farnham in Surrey wrote to the Post Office asking for one to be installed in her flat. She received the following reply:

> Dear Customer,
> Thank you for your application for telephone service. I have tried to contact you by telephone without success. . . .

For officials, the problem can be in deciding when to stop. There is a notice at the entrance of a Government building in London which reads:

> Maximum width seven feet. All vehicles exceeding this width are prohibited from entering these gates.

The motive, at least, is understandable: somebody wants to tell me something and I know what it is. But one of the mysteries of our language is how words, simple to understand individually, can become meaningless when put together. Pity the poor 'A' level examiners who had to wrestle with the official advice:

> Results will be indicated by points on a scale derived linearly from the examiners' marks, but truncated at either end so as to be of uniform length in all cases.

And just in case the message hasn't quite got home:

> In terms of any scale on which the results are recorded, users should consider that a candidate's true level of attainment in each subject, while possibly represented by a scale point one or two higher or lower, is more likely to be represented by the scale point awarded than by any other scale point.

Which perhaps goes some way to explaining why exam results are so capricious. *The Financial Times* recently told the story of the stockbroker's son who had worked very hard for his 'O' levels. Great things were expected of him, so even greater was the disappointment when he failed everything except Religious Instruction and Woodwork. The disgruntled father, when asked what his son was going to do, replied: 'I don't know. Carve pulpits, I suppose.'

But without examinations there could be nothing for the examiners to mess up. Knowing that the passing of examinations is the whole purpose of education today, some students at an engineering firm stumbled on a fundamental fault. It's not the students who are too dim, it's the exams that are too hard. So they devised their own; pass mark was 40%.

1. What language is spoken by French Canadians?
2. Give the important characteristics of the ancient Babylonian Empire, with particular reference to architecture, literature, law and social services.
   OR give the names of The Beatles.
3. What religion is the Pope?
   Jewish/Catholic/Hindu or Anglican?
4. Would you ask William Shakespeare to build a bridge/sail the ocean/lead an army or write a play?
5. What is a Silver dollar made of?
6. What time is it when the big hand is on the One and the little hand is on the Twelve?
7. How many commandments (approximately) was Moses given?
8. Spell.... London, Dublin, Kenton and Sussex.
9. What country is the Queen of England Queen of?
10. What are the people who live in England's North called? Easterners/Westerners/Southerners/Northerners?
    Underline one only.

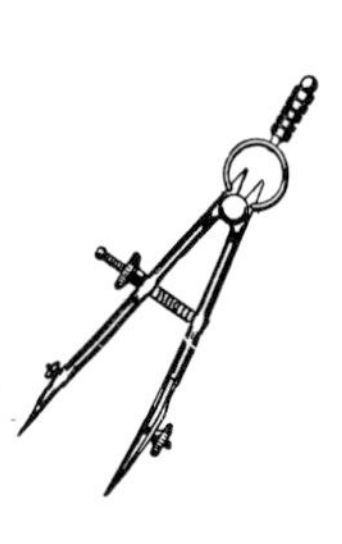

11. Six Kings of England have been called George, the last one being George VI. Name the previous five.
12. Who won World War II? Who came second?
13. Where does the rain come from? Supermarket/Harrods/USA/The Sky?
14. Who invented STEPHENSON'S ROCKET? Winston Churchill/Fanny Cradock/George Stephenson.
15. Can you explain Einstein's Theory of Relativity? Yes or No?
16. The song 'O Canada' is the National Anthem of what country?
17. Explain Le Chatelier's Principle of Equilibrium Force.
    OR spell your last name in block letters.
18. What holiday falls on January 1st? Christmas/New Year or Thanksgiving? One only.
19. What is a coat hanger?
20. Where is the basement in a three-storey building?

We need exams like that if we are to produce the positive, clean-thinking people needed for the world of today. Leaders of men – leaders to draft orders for the rest of us to follow. This is an extract from a British Admiralty instruction:

> It is necessary for technical reasons that these warheads should be stored with the top at the bottom and the bottom at the top. In order that there may be no doubt which is the bottom for storage purposes, it will be seen that the bottom of each head has been labelled with the word TOP.

And from the National Insurance Bill, 1st Schedule:

> For the purpose of this part of this schedule a person over pensionable age, not being an insured person, shall be treated as an employed person if he would be an insured person were he under pensionable age and would be an employed person were he an insured person.

But it's amazing what can be achieved by the injection of a little humour, even in the sorry business of debt chasing. A friend in Leicester received this letter about an overdue account:

> OVERDUE ACCOUNT
> We address you, Dear Sirs, as a debtor
> But rather than write a rude letter
> We choose to suppose
> That you knows what you owes
> And the sooner you pays it the better.

He replied in similar vein:

> OVERDUE ACCOUNT
> We acknowledge, Dear Sirs, your letter
> Concerning our dues as a debtor
> You will be pleased to know
> We have sent you the dough
> Our relations should now be much better.

ACCOUNT
DEPT.
STATEMENT
FINAL REQUEST

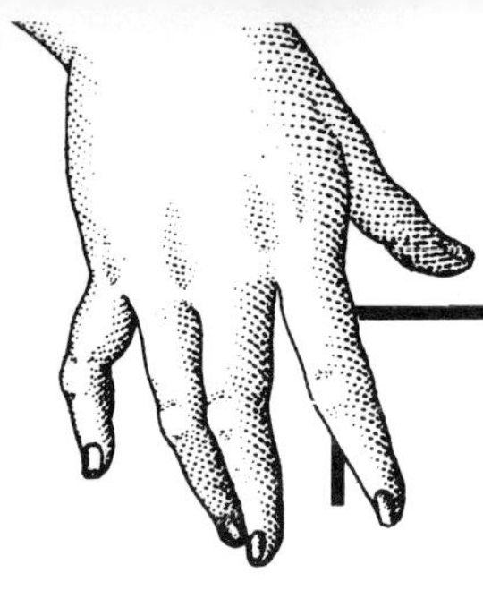

Children Start Early

BIRTH

YALDEN – to Michael and Janet (née Read) on May 29th 1972 at Mount Alvernia, Guildford, a son (Richard James Read), brother and demolition partner for John.

When the Duke of Windsor was asked for his impression of America he is reported to have replied: 'I think it's the way parents obey the children.' But don't we all? Everyone who has a child to obey has at least one story to tell. I asked for them and I got them. Many concerned words and their use of them:

A little girl, walking with her mother, on spying an oil slick on top of a puddle, was heard to say: 'Look Mummy, there's a dead rainbow.'

And:

After a school trip to the zoo the children were told to write about their favourite animal in the zoo. One little girl wrote: The Animal that interested me most was the WARNING STAND BACK. Every time we looked at him, he spat at us.

Or the confusing way we use them:

On her first day at school, little Debbie began to cry. 'You aren't homesick, are you?' asked the teacher kindly. 'NO,' was the tearful response. 'I'm *here* sick.'

Or what a confusing place school is:

A small girl was pointing out to her teacher that 2 + 2 doesn't always equal four. 'Two raindrops plus two raindrops make a puddle.'

And talking of puddles:

When Queen Elizabeth I stepped on Sir Walter Raleigh's cloak to cross a big puddle she turned to Sir Walter and said: 'I'm afraid I have dirtied your cloak, Sir Walter.' To which he replied: 'Dieu et mon droit,' which means 'My God you're right.' (Child's essay)

The idea of God has always caused problems:

Passing a church, my five-year-old nephew asked: 'Who lives there?' I told him God did. He peered through the door and in the windows back and front, then came back to report: 'I can't see him, but I know he's there 'cos his bike's around the back.'

To say nothing of the problems caused by His ambassadors:

At Sunday lunch at the vicarage there was no knife, fork or spoon for the visiting bishop. 'Why,' asked the Vicar's wife of her six-year-old daughter, 'haven't you laid his place correctly?' 'Oh, he doesn't need cutlery,' the child replied. 'Daddy says he eats like a horse.'

Children can be very hard to impress:

A six-year-old girl was on her first visit to the circus. She was spellbound watching the tight-rope walker. 'Isn't it exciting to see the lady run across that little wire,' said her mother. 'Oh,' said the little girl, awfully let down. 'Is there a wire? I thought she was walking on air.'

But they want to know things:

> A young lecturer, aware of the awkward questions children are liable to ask, mugged up on every last detail of information about otters before he faced the kids at the local primary school. He even borrowed a stuffed otter from the museum. He then presented his talk cramming in the maximum of information. Having finished he sat back and asked for questions. Immediately a child's hand shot up.
> 'Yes,' said the lecturer.
> Pointing at the otter, the child asked: 'What is it stuffed with?'

And they have such logical brains:

> Youngest son: 'Mum, does the Queen go to Ascot?'
> Mum: 'Yes, that's why it's called Royal Ascot.'
> Dad: 'It's Royal Ascot for the first four days because the Queen's there. On Saturday she doesn't go and then it's called Ascot Heath.'
> Daughter: 'Oh! Does Ted Heath go then?'

But it's that same logic that can make them so lovable:

> When the manager of a firm rang one of his salesmen at home the telephone was answered by a small boy. 'May I speak to your father?' asked the manager.
> 'Daddy isn't home,' replied the small boy.
> 'Well is there anyone else I could speak to?'
> 'There's my sister,' said the boy.
> 'Well, could I speak to her, then?'
> There followed a long pause, then the boy's voice was heard again.
> 'Sorry,' he said. 'I can't lift her out of the playpen.'

A Small Load of Cobblers

We talk about 'putting on your shoes and socks'. Why? Who puts on their shoes before their socks?

We tell people to 'wipe their feet'. Why? We really want them to wipe their shoes.

There are many superstitions about shoes, more often bad than good:

New shoes, when you bring them home, should never be placed on a shelf higher than your head (bad luck).

Don't drop them before they've been worn (bad luck).

Don't clean them before you've had both shoes on (even worse luck).

As for habits while wearing the things:

Shoes worn at the toes – he spends as he goes.

Shoes worn at the side – she'll be a rich man's bride.

If you've a mother in Germany, don't lose a heel; you will also lose one of your children before the year is out.

The only good bit of news on the footwear front concerns old shoes. Keep your old shoes because they bring good luck.

If your laces keep coming untied, your loved one is thinking about you.

To cure a head cold, throw an old shoe on the fire (why isn't that bad luck?) and inhale the smoke.

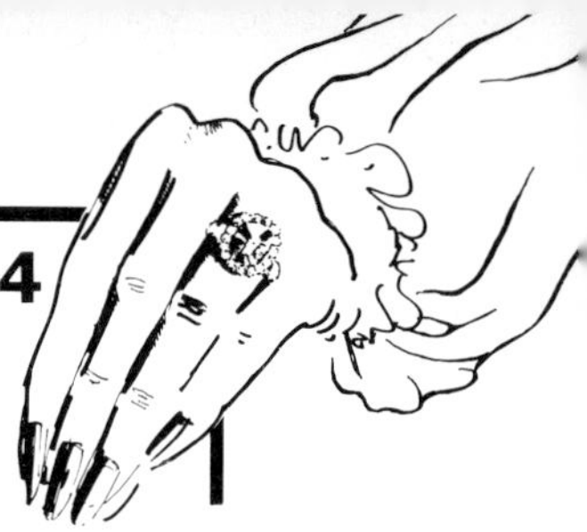

Chapter 4

She Sells Sea Shells

Tonguetwisters are a broadcaster's nightmare. I remember the Christmas Eve news story about the turkeys that had been given away at Smithfield meat market. Old age pensioners had carried off 'free freshly plucked turkeys.' I've also run foul of the 'Port Talbot tin-plate plant'; from space 'Soyuz Six seems certain to make a soft surface landing.' The microphone got equally wet with 'Six Swedish fishing-smacks sank in the Skagerrak last night.' So how are we broadcasters supposed to regard those people who dream them up deliberately?

Peter Piper and his peck of pickled peppers has nothing on this:

> Theophilus Thistle the unsifted thistle sifter sifted a sieve full of unsifted thistles. If Theophilus Thistle the unsifted thistle sifter sifted a sieve full of unsifted thistles what became of the sieve full of unsifted thistles Theophilus Thistle the unsifted thistle sifter sifted?

That pattern for a tonguetwister probably goes back to the very earliest examples. Some of the oldest were contained in a book called *Peter Piper's Practical Principles of Plain and Perfect Pronunciation*, published in 1834. Here are a couple:

Oliver Oglethorpe ogled an owl and oyster.
Did Oliver Oglethorpe ogle an owl and oyster?
If Oliver Oglethorpe ogled an owl and oyster,
Where are the owl and oyster Oliver
Oglethorpe ogled?

Captain Crackskull cracked a catchpoll's
cockscomb.
Did Captain Crackskull crack a catchpoll's
cockscomb?
If Captain Crackskull cracked a catchpoll's
cockscomb
Where's the catchpoll's cockscomb Captain
Crackskull cracked?

And to this day tonguetwisters are alive and well and living in every school in the land:

A school coal scuttle, a scuttle of school coal.

Three thousand, three hundred and thirty-three
feathers down a thrush's throat.

I'm not a pheasant plucker
I'm the pheasant plucker's mate
I'm only plucking pheasants
'Cos the pheasant plucker's late!

(If you find yourself saying the word 'pleasant', stop at once!)

If a Hottentot tot taught a Hottentot tot to
talk 'ere that tot could totter, should the
Hottentot tot be taught to say aught, or naught,
or what ought to be taught her?

A tutor who tooted the flute
Tried to tutor two tooters to toot
Said the two to the tutor
Is it harder to toot, or
To tutor two tooters to toot?

There's no need to light a night-light
On a light night like tonight
For a night-light is a slight light
On a light night like tonight.

Betty Bolter bought some butter
'But,' she said, 'this butter's bitter!
If I put it in my batter
It will make my batter bitter
Better than the bitter batter
That will make my batter butter better!'

So she bought a bit of butter
Better than the bitter butter
And made her batter butter better
So 'twas better Betty Bolter
Bought a bit of better butter
For her better batter butter.

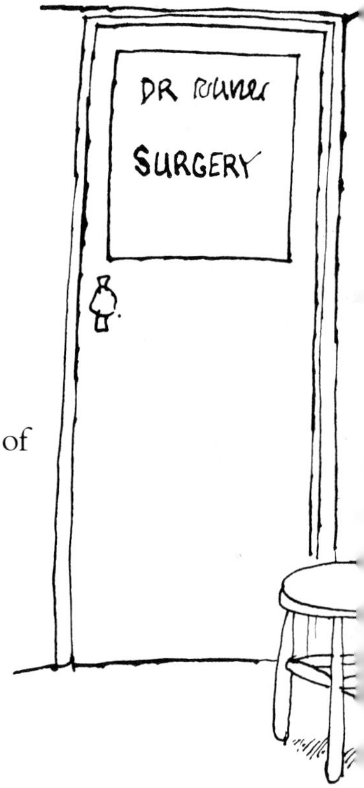

Tonguetwisters are intended to bring on an acute attack of glottal dislocation, but some actually have a purpose. This is how sheep are counted in the North of England:

Yan = 1
Tan = 2
Tethera = 3
Pethera = 4
Pip = 5
Sethera = 6
Lethera = 7
Howra = 8
Dowra = 9
Dik = 10
Yanadik = 11
Tanadik = 12
Tetherkik = 13
Petheradik = 14
Bumfit = 15
Yanabumfit = 16
Tanabumfit = 17
Tetherabumfit = 18
Petherabumfit = 19
Jigget = 20

There is even what we might call a mental tonguetwister. The challenge here is to make sense of a sentence that includes a sequence of the word 'had'. Punctuate please!

Smith where Jones had had had had had had had had had had had the examiner's approval.

(Answer: Smith, where Jones had had 'had', had had 'had had'. 'Had had' had had the examiner's approval.)

I'll give you the punctuation here. We might call this Dormant Difficulties, but it shows again just how complex is our language:

> A sleeper is one who sleeps. A sleeper is that in which the sleeper sleeps. A sleeper is that on which the sleeper runs while the sleeper sleeps. Therefore, while the sleeper sleeps in the sleeper, the sleeper carries the sleeper over the sleeper under the sleeper, until the sleeper which carries the sleeper jumps the sleeper and wakes the sleeper in the sleeper by striking the sleeper on the sleeper and there is no longer any sleeper sleeping in the sleeper on the sleeper.

We've also tried to find the longest recorded spoken sentence. I think that was won by Mr Gladstone in a speech he delivered in Birmingham which began:

> Sir Charles Forster and Gentlemen, it is a great thing and a great praise to any constituency that it is able to maintain that standard of judgment and approbation and attachment which Walsall has maintained for so long a period while represented by Sir Charles Forster, to whom I owe a debt of gratitude for what he has most truly called an unswerving support, but I may say a support that did not derive its entire value even from its singularly decided character in reference to the principle of Liberalism, but likewise from the entire character and action of the man who has been successful in making Liberal principles honoured by the whole House in association with active parliamentary service rendered to the House of Commons as such, without respect to party, while at the same time he has been one no doubt, as he had said himself, of the most intelligent upholders of the principles of party as being a necessary, though secondary, instrument for promoting the benefit of the work and the empire.

At which point he should have sat down exhausted. A sentence of 175 words!

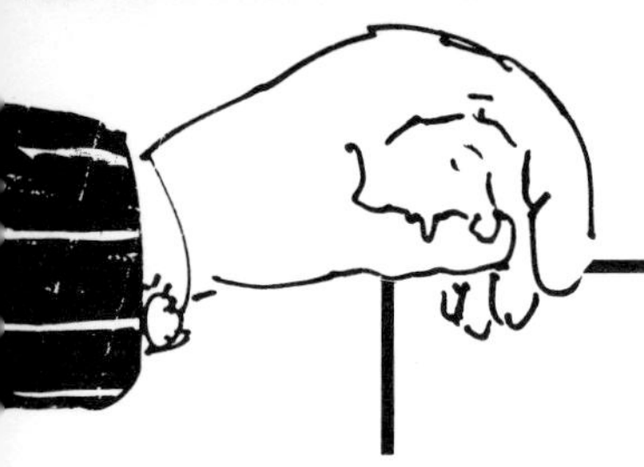

Chapter 5

Dear P45

The word 'computer' doesn't even appear in my dictionary (circa 1953), and yet there is a widely held belief that they are here to stay. But do they improve efficiency? Perhaps you should ask the employees of Avon County Council. They installed a computer in 1975 which started by paying a caretaker £75 an hour instead of 75p an hour, paid another £2,600 for a week's work and ended up at the centre of a strike. A protest meeting was called attended by 280 employees of whom only eight had been paid the correct salary.

A computer making human errors is one thing. To attempt also to give it a human face is surely unforgiveable. Patients at American hospitals who don't pay up promptly get the following letter:

> Hello there!
> I am the hospital's computer. As yet no one but me knows that you have not been making regular payments on this account. However, if I have not processed a payment from you within 10 days, I will tell a human who will resort to other means of collection.

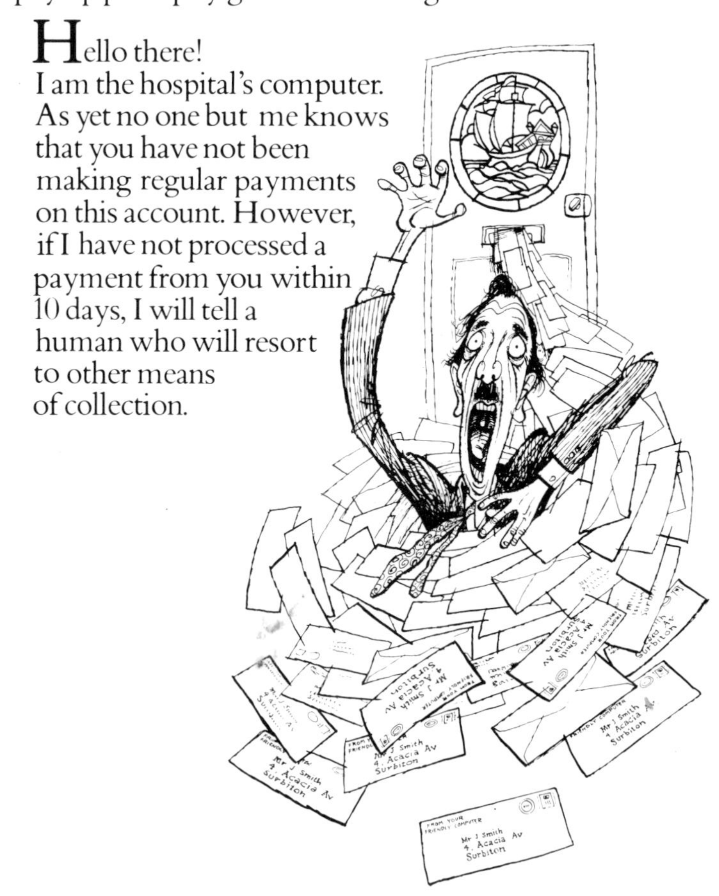

Which is a real breakthrough for human relations. But having machines that behave like humans must be expected; after all, for years we've encouraged humans to behave like machines. I am thinking of the Inland Revenue. Occasionally, however, a wintry smile can almost be seen to crack across the Inspector's face, and when that happens, like the first cuckoo, listeners find it worth reporting.

A Liverpool man was so angry that his tax problems were not being sorted out that he cut the two pockets from his trousers and sent them to the local Tax Office with a note that said:

> You may as well have them, you've left me nothing to fill them.

H.M. INSPECTOR OF TAXES
6 APR 1982

Back came the reply:

> Dear Sir,
> Your code number will be amended. I trust you will partly fill your pockets now.

(Note the use of the word 'partly'. Surely, only the taxman would be so mean-spirited.)

Then there was the man from Stevenage, Hertfordshire, who listed as 'Dependent Relatives' H Wilson and R Jenkins, who were then respectively Prime Minister and Chancellor of the Exchequer. The reply came back:

> Having examined fully your claim, we consider the relationship to be too distant to allow you to be eligible for the allowance.

But income tax is not something that many people find very amusing. Such humour as there is, tends to be unintentional. These extracts are from letters sent to the Inland Revenue (and later leaked to us by a 'mole'):

> Re your request for P45 for new employee. You already have it and he isn't leaving here but coming, so we haven't got it.

> I hereby appeal on the grounds that your estimate is based on chickens counted before they are hatched. (From a poultry keeper)

Thank you for explaining my income tax liability. You have done it so clearly that I almost understand it.

My husband died on November 3rd. Is there any post-war credit due as I understand a person has to die before receiving any benefit.

I have to inform you that my mother-in-law passed away after receiving your form on November 22nd. Thanking you.

I received your IT form but had to go into hospital an hour afterwards.

I have not been living with my husband for several years, and have much pleasure in enclosing his last will and testament.

Please correct this assessment. I have not worked for the past three months, as I have broken my leg. Hoping you will do the same.

I cannot pay the full amount at the moment as my husband is in hospital. As soon as I can, I will send on the remains.

My husband is in HM Forces. I have no children. Trusting it will have your attention.

Please send me a claim form as I have had a baby. I had one before but it got dirty and I burnt it.

I am writing to inform you that I am now married. I realize I should have done so eight months ago, but I wasn't aware that I had to.

I am a vermin destroyer, but I have not earned anything for a month. I shall be glad to call on you at any time.

It is said that among the numerous forms to be filled in by applicants to the staff of the Inland Revenue is one that asks:

Number of children (by sex)

One answer read:

Two. And one by adoption.

Do not forget, no matter how sincere and open your letter may be, you can expect only low cunning from the other side. A taxpayer in Philadelphia received a very strongly worded Second Demand, telling him his taxes were overdue. He hurried down to the tax office to pay his bill in person and remarked apologetically that he must have overlooked the First Demand. With that universal wintry smile the man said: 'Ah, but didn't you know, we no longer send out First Demands. We've found that Second Demands are so much more effective.'

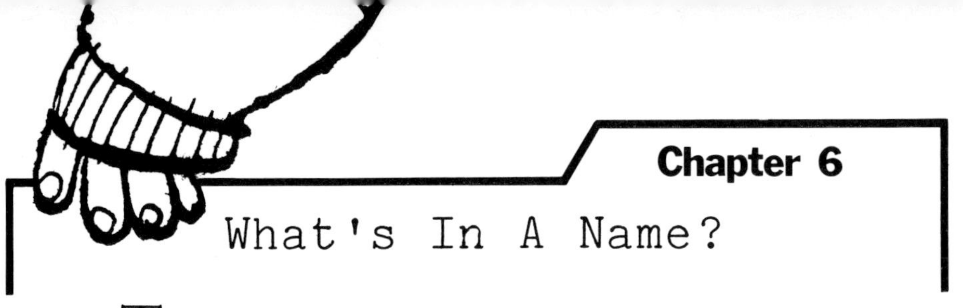

Chapter 6

What's In A Name?

The Bard was wrong. When you get down to it, *everything* is in a name. Roses might smell nice under new management, but you try selling a bottle of perfume without a label such as Chanel, Givenchy, etc. Or an unsigned picture, or a book by an unknown author. Conversely, is junk really junk if it comes in a Harrods bag? Names are profoundly important, and it's not surprising to discover how much they have influenced our lives – even in the choice of career. Take

I A Screech
Dental Surgeon

Could Mr Screech have been anything else? There's another dentist, also in the Reading area, called Mr Pullar – presumably a more physical chap. Similarly, Mr J H Smellie was always destined to be a Public Health Inspector, Mr Clogg a surgical shoemaker, Mr Bee a superintendent of Parks and Gardens, and Mr T O Pincher the area sales manager of a shoe company.

For them, it is clearly all preordained. With others, External Fate takes a hand:

> When it was reported to Warminster Police 'that a body was being transferred from one van to another under cover of darkness', it was somehow inevitable that 'PC Coffin was sent to investigate'.

> And when students at the Technical College, Colchester claimed a leap-frogging record of 15 miles they were 'under the direction of lecturer Mr Gerald Jump'.

> So, too, after Newhall Ebenezer Young Wives had been given 'a most informative talk on family planning', it seemed only natural that 'the next speaker on June 2nd will be Mr Gotobed, the Public Health Inspector'.

For some, the best advice is: stay away from lawyers.

> An American lawyer was introduced to a man named Versus. 'You married, Mr Versus?' he asked. 'No,' said Mr Versus. 'Why?' 'Well, if you were married,' replied the lawyer, 'and wanted a divorce, I'd handle the case free just for the hell of filing Versus versus Versus!'

It's hardly surprising that some 'names' should band together for mutual comfort. For example, at Bertram Ramsey Further Education Centre in Middlesbrough:

> Mr Brewer teaches winemaking and Mr Fixter presides over the modelling class. Keep-fit and games are run by Mr Sturdy and the metalwork classes are the province of Mr Steele. Woodwork and cabinetmaking are classes run by Mr Woodhouse and finally the basketry and canework teacher is none other than Mr Stringer. A spokesman for Teesside Education Department said: 'It is entirely coincidental.'

Occasionally, Fate plans a meeting so that a business partnership can be born:

Argue and Phibbs – Solicitors, Albert Street, Sligo

Fidler & Leake – London's Roofing Specialists

Rippin, Bangs & Partners – Estate Agents

So far we've dealt only with surnames. You have only to look down the personal columns of the newspapers to see that some of us don't make life any easier for our children with the first names we give them:

BOTTOM – To Mavis and Donald (safety officer), a daughter Patricia Anne... (Pat A Bottom)

OCHS – On Jan 25 to Annie and Robin Ochs, a daughter, a sister for Olly and Daisy... (Olly Ochs!)

And for those with longer memories – when money was money:

Miss Farthing married Mr Penny and produced a son called 'Bob'.

Can anyone still question the link between a person's name and lifestyle? If so, here are some more:

Mr J Fox lecturers on 'The Care of Furs'
Elsie Codd – Agent for Finbarr Sea Food
J H Wellburn – Coal Merchant
A Killer – High Class Baker and Confectioner
D R Gatherum – Apple Grower
Maurice Snipper – Tailor
Kenneth MacVicar – Parish Minister
'The Gift of Eternal Life' – Speaker, Mr A L Deadman
Edna D Fudge – Proprietor of 'The Candy Store'
Trueperch Ltd – L E Bird, Director

Some apparently unremarkable names have made such an impact that they have passed into the language. 'Before you can say Jack Robinson' and 'Bob's Your Uncle' are two examples. But who were Jack Robinson and Bob? They did exist:

> A certain John Robinson was born in Appleby, in Westmorland, in 1727 and became mayor in 1760 and then entered Parliament and was the Secretary of the Treasury. The famous saying is said to have come from the dramatist Sheridan, who was an MP and during a debate made allegations of bribery against the administration. Members called out for the name of the culprit and Sheridan, gazing at John Robinson, replied with great point: 'Yes, I could name him as soon as I could say Jack Robinson.'

As for Bob:

He was Lord Salisbury (Robert Arthur Talbot Gascoyne Cecil) who became Prime Minister in 1885. When Arthur Balfour, a comparatively unknown MP, was appointed Chief Secretary in 1886, it was noted that the Prime Minister was his Uncle Bob. People suspected favouritism – and thus the phrase 'Bob's Your Uncle' was coined.

Finally, who would argue with these wise sayings?

A person with a bad name is already half-hanged. (Old Proverb)

The first Rotarian was the first man to call John the Baptist, Jack. (H L Mencken)

A man's name is a perfectly fitting garment which like the skin has grown over him and at which one cannot rake or scrape without injuring the man himself. (Goethe)

Names are not always what they seem. The common Welsh name BZJXXLLWCP is pronounced Jackson. (Mark Twain)

Chapter 7

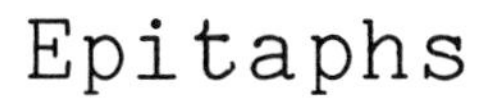

Epitaphs

Now that the nation's graveyards are almost full up (and none of those old jokes about 'standing room only'), the tombstone with ample space for several lines of epitaph is becoming a thing of the past. Already it has been supplanted in many churchyards by those much smaller tablets that sprout in gardens of remembrance. Time, then, to recall the more spacious days when a four-line poem beneath the name and dates was no great extravagance – even if the message was sometimes a bit rumbustious for present-day sensibilities:

> Here lie I and my four daughters
> Who died of drinking Cheltenham waters;
> If we had stuck to Epsom salts,
> We wouldn't be lying in these here vaults.

Who actually wrote that? you wonder. Surely not the old boy himself, the 'I' of the poem. (Or was the 'I' the mother?) How would they have had time? Perhaps a kindly relative decided that something jolly best fitted the family, then either composed the lines or called in some 'poetical person' to do the job. That's the trouble with epitaphs: if you don't write your own, or get it done while you're alive, you have to put your faith entirely in others, for there's no way they can get a draft to you for approval once you're six feet under. And even your best friends don't always hit quite the right note. From Edinburgh I received this:

> Erected to the memory of John Macfarlane,
> Drown'd in the water of the river
> by a few friends.

And from Woolwich churchyard:

> Sacred to the memory of Major James Brush
> who was killed by the accidental discharge
> of his pistol by his orderly 14th April 1831.
> Well done good and faithful servant.

Another problem with using other writers is that they may start tinkering with your reputation – in the nicest possible way, of course:

> Here lies the body of Mary Shaw
> Born a virgin, she died a whore
> For sixteen years she kept her virginity
> Which established a record for this vicinity.

The vicinity, by the way, was Caernarvon. But not to worry, up there in North Wales: I've seen a very similar epitaph from Aberdeen (strange, the fashions people follow).

But while it must be better to write your own epitaph, what should you put? Best not to blow your own trumpet too much. At the other extreme, how about this for an example of modesty, brevity, and the sense of comedy that makes it memorable:

> Almighty God
> If there is one
> Have mercy on my soul
> If I have one.

Finally, a tribute to that most ancient of community servants, the local gravedigger:

> The graves around for many a year
> Were dug by he who slumbers here
> 'Til worn with age he dropped his spade
> And in the dust his bones were laid.

Chapter 8

Eggheads Of The World, Unite!

You have nothing to lose but your yolks
(Adlai Stevenson)

I used to be the nation's alarm clock in the days before Terry Wogan. ('How Terry-ble to be a Wogan like that,' some wit remarked at the change-over.) A frequent accusation made against me was that I was hitting people when they were down by challenging them to solve puzzles before their feet had even hit the ground. Well, either my wits have slowed or I ought to go back to getting up at 4 am, because some of the puzzles now seem impossibly difficult, particularly when you remember that the people on the receiving end were being 'talked at' and couldn't read the questions for themselves.

All I can do is offer my apologies and resurrect a few in print. Take as much time as you like.

My watch is ten minutes slow and I think that it is five minutes fast. Your watch is five minutes fast and you think that it is ten minutes slow. We plan to catch a train that departs at four o'clock. Who gets there first?

Answer You get there first and I miss the train. Thinking that my watch is five minutes fast I will try to arrive for 4.05 by my watch. In fact it is ten minutes slow so I arrive at 4.15 correct time and miss the train. You think that your watch is ten minutes slow and will arrive for 3.50 by your watch which is 3.45 correct time.

Make 1000 by using only eight 8s.
Answer 8 plus 8 plus 8 plus 88 plus 888 = 1000.

Three men have 90 oranges to sell between them. One has 50, another 30 and the third 10. However, they all end up with the same amount of money and they all sell them at the same rate. How?
Answer They sell them at the (admittedly rather absurd) rate of 7 for 1p with any over being sold off at 3p each. So they all end up with 10p.

Complete the following sequence: $\frac{1}{4}$, $\frac{1}{2}$, 1, 3, 6, 12, 24.
Answer 30. Remember old money? The next in the sequence is the half-crown, or 30 pence.

It's a celebration. Three women have two daughters each and they all go out for a meal in a restaurant. 'Good Evening, Mesdames,' says the head waiter. 'A table for 7? Certainly, come this way.' And he hadn't miscounted. Why only 7, please?
Answer One of the women is the grandmother.

Her two daughters are the mothers of the 4 other daughters. So the family dinner party consists of 7 people.

You have 8 coins in your hand (10p or similar). The object is to get them down on the table in the sequence heads, tails, heads, tails, etc. The puzzle is how the coins must be arranged in your hand if only alternate coins are put on the table, the intervening ones being slid back under the pile, ie one coin on the table, one to the bottom of the stack, one on the table, etc.
Answer Heads, heads, tails, heads, heads, tails, tails, tails.

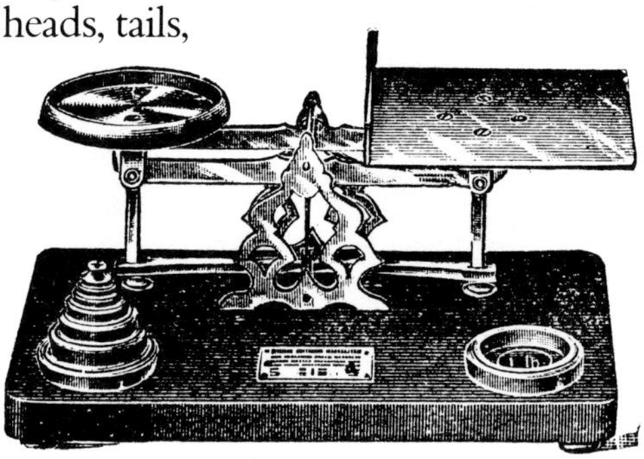

Which is heavier, a pound of gold or a pound of potatoes?
Answer A pound of potatoes. Gold is measured by Troy weight and potatoes by avoirdupois – which is nearly 22% heavier than a Troy pound.

But not all the puzzles concern numbers.

Name a 7-letter word with no vowels.
Answer Rhythms.

There are 78 ways to say somebody is left-handed. How many do you know?
Answer Back-handed, ballock-handed, bang-handed, bang-hand, bawky-handed, buck-fisted, cack-handed, cacky, caggy, caggy-fisted, caggy-handed, cam-fisted, car-handed, car-pawed, cat-handed, cawk-fisted, cawk-handed, click, clicky, clicky-handed, cob-handed, cock-handed, coochy-gammy, coochy-handed, cowly-handed, cow-pawed, dollock-handed, dolly-pawed, gallock-handed, gally-handed, gammy-fisted, gammy-handed, gammy-palmed, gawk-handed, gawky-handed, gawp-handed, gibble-fisted, golly-handed, kay-fisted, kay-fist, kay-neive, kay-neived, kay-pawed, keck-fisted, keck-handed, kecky-fisted, kecky-handed, keg-handed, keg-pawed, keggy, kittagh-hand, kittaghy, left-caggy, left-cooch,

left-cooched, left-hand, left-handed, left-keg, left-kegged, left-keggy, left-kelly, left-plug, marlborough-handed, north-handed, scoochy, scroochy, scram-handed, scrammy-handed, skiffy, skiffy-handed, skivvy-handed, south-pawed, squiffy, squippy, squiver-handed, watted, watty, watty-handed.

Among the derivations for left-handed, 'car' is of Scandinavian origin, 'kay' is Danish, 'cuddy' is English, and 'clicky' and 'coochy' are possibly Celtic. 'Cack' and its derivatives are terms of abuse (meaning excreta). 'Marlborough-handed' comes from the name of the Wiltshire town, where they used to regard left-handed people as idiots. 'South-pawed' comes from the USA and 'north-handed' has presumably been inverted from this.

Source: Prof H Orton, *Survey of English Dialects*.

Who are the well-known people in these anagrams?

Hated for Ill
Won half the new world's glory
He'll do in mellow verse
Flit on! Cheering angel
Our best novelist, senor

Answers Adolf Hitler, Henry Wadsworth Longfellow, Oliver Wendell Holmes, Florence Nightingale, Robert Louis Stevenson.

And while on anagrams, who is:

The warm lion *or* Woman Hitler
Answer Mother-in-law.

But not all these morning headaches were puzzles. Some were simply games:

Write down your age, double it, add 5, multiply by 50, subtract 365, add the number of coins in your pocket or purse. Add 115. The first two figures will give your age, the last two your coins.

Or variations on the same theme:

> Open a book at random and pick a word within the first 10 lines and within the 10th word from the end of the line. Now – double the number of the page and multiply by 5. Add 20. Add the number of the chosen line. Add 5. Multiply by 10 and add the number of the chosen word in the line. Subtract 250 and the sum is finished. The unit figure is the number of the word. In the ten column is the number of the line. The remaining figures are the number of the page.
>
> The number 987654321 is interesting. Multiply it by 45 and you get 44,444,444,445. Turn it round the other way, to 123456789, again multiply by 45, and you get 5,555,555,505.

Then we had some spelling curiosities, such as:

> What does 'Ghoti' spell?
> *Answer* Fish GH – as in Cough F
> O – as in Women I
> TI – as in Station SH
> (Thanks to G B Shaw)

Now you've got the hang of it, try this:

> What does 'Ghoughpatheightteeau' spell?
> *Answer* Potato GH – as in Hiccough P
> OUGH – as in Dough O
> PATH – as in Pathisis T
> EIGH – as in Neighbour A
> TTE – as in Gazette T
> EAU – as in Beau O

Obviously, looking back, I took a sadistic pleasure in ruining other people's mornings – mine having been ruined already! Imagine trying to keep up with this before you even knew which day it was!

> A man from Pennsylvania was reported to have committed suicide because he was convinced that he was his own grandfather. Here's the letter he left behind:

I married a widow who had a grown-up daughter. My father visited our house very often, fell in love with my step-daughter, and married her. So my father became my son-in-law and my step-daughter my mother, because she was my father's wife. Some time afterwards my wife had a son; he was my father's brother-in-law and my uncle, for he was the brother of my step-mother. My father's wife, ie my step-daughter, had also a son; he was, of course, my brother, and in the meantime my grandchild, for he was the son of my daughter. My wife was my grandmother, because she was my mother's mother. I was my wife's husband and grandchild at the same time. And as the husband of a person's grandmother is his grandfather, I was my own grandfather.

Let his bones and our brains rest in peace! As for eggheads and philsophers, a plague on the lot of them! Is it not true that:

If everybody contemplated the infinite instead of fixing their drains – many of us are going to die of cholera. (John Rich)

The greatest lesson in life is to know that even fools are right sometimes. (Winston Churchill)

A Master of Art
Is not worth a fart
(Andrew Boorde, 16th century)

If a man empties his purse into his head – no one can take it from him. (Benjamin Franklin)

Education is the process of casting false pearls before real swines. (Irwin Edman)

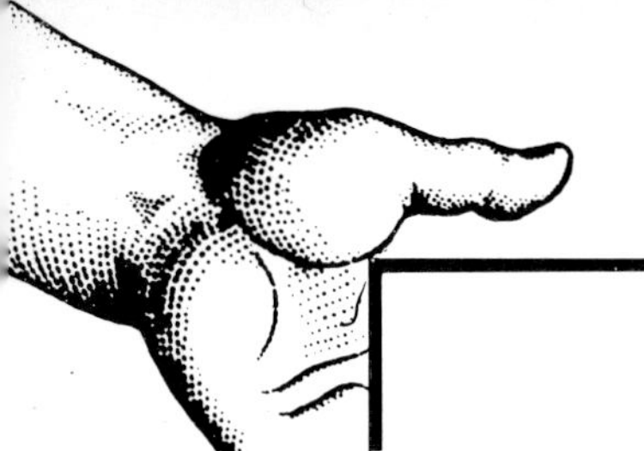

Chapter 9

The A-to-Z Game

So you know the A-to-Z game? I warn you, it can become addictive! A 26-word sentence, each word to start with the next letter of the alphabet in sequence.

> A blonde called Dora entertained friends generously. Her indecent jokes kept luring men near; only police, quite rightly, stopped these undesirable vices with extraordinary youthful zeal.

> Able bodied conscientious dustmen emptying filthy garbage handle indescribable junk. Kitchen leftovers make noxious odours producing quite revolting stenches. This unwholesome vegetation won't exactly yield zeal.

Yes, we got a lot of 'zeal' – and what about 'zest'?

> After Billy caught Diana excitedy filling George's huge imbibing jug, Kenneth let more nectar overflow, pouring quantities rather stupidly through Uncle's vest whilst xylophonists yodelled zestfully.

But there were also plenty of other 'z' words:

> African Broadcasting Corporations deny elephants form great herds in jungles killing lions, maiming natives or pursuing quarries relentlessly suddenly trampling underfoot very wild, excited young zebras.

> A bear cub drowsily eats flesh, greedily his iron jaws keep lacerating meat, noticeably of poor quality. Resulting serious tummy upset very worrying, explains young zoologist.

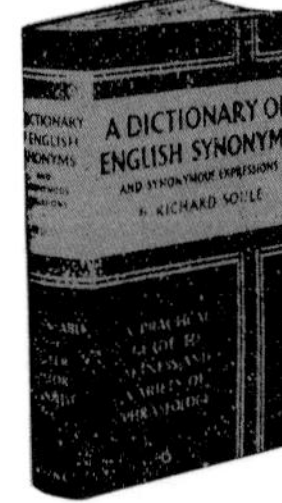

As if that wasn't difficult enough, someone even turned the whole thing into a history lesson. Thus, a summary of Old Testament chronology:

> Adam begat Cain (1) David effectually fought Goliath (2) Hilkiah in Jerusalem kept lawbooks (3) many noble old prophets queried royal standards (4) too, until violent warriors exiled young Zedekiah (5).
> (1) Gen 4.1, (2) 1 Sam 17, (3) 2 Kings 22.8, (4) 2 Sam, (5) 2 Kings 25.7

While others saw double:

> Arthur Askey, benign, benevolent comedy character, drove deftly every evening from Fulham going gaily homeward. His interest in jokers' jests kept keen lively little men merry. Nevertheless, nearly outside own porch, police quickly questioned roamer's return saying suavely that their useful usually varied vigilant watch was exceedingly exceptional yielding young Zionist Zulu.

And once started, some couldn't stop:

> After breakfast Colin drove extremely fast, guiding his immaculate Jaguar keenly Londonwards. Much nervous overtaking posed questions regarding safety. Though unusual vibration was experienced, yet, zooming along blisteringly, Colin dozed. Expectedly fate's grim hand intervened. Juddering, knocking large metal nuts off prolifically, quick return shaft twisted. Unheeding violent warnings, expected years zero, airborne briefly, Colin dreadfully expired!

I said you could get hooked. Why don't you try? Not that it's such a new idea: in 1842 *The Times* printed this version:

> To widowers and single gentlemen. Wanted by a lady, a situation to superintend the household and preside at table. She is agreeable, becoming, careful, deniable, English, facetious, generous, honest, industrious, judicious, keen, lively, merry, natty, obedient, philosophic, quiet, regular, sociable, tasteful, useful, vivacious, womanish, xantippish, youthful, zealous. Address: Simmonds Library, Edgware Road.

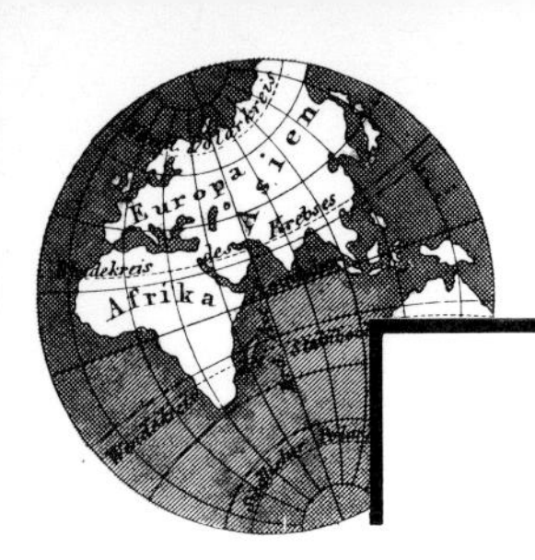

Chapter 10
It's A Small World

Everyone is intrigued by coincidences – if that is what they are. Sometimes the odds are so long or the meetings so strange, one wonders. I have always tried to resist any suggestions of the supernatural: 'Nature caught in the act of rhyming' is how I like to think of them. Here are just a few of the many personal stories that have been sent to me.

In 1963 I was only 18 and was serving in the Anti-Submarine Frigate HMS *Whirlwind* stationed in the West Indies. And she was well-named because our job was to follow behind the hurricanes that frequently devastated that area towards the end of summer. We sailed close behind this monster of nature to offer help to any of the small islands unfortunate enough to have suffered damage. We had a secondary task too – we carried out beach landings in the middle of the night on any islands suspected of harbouring Cuban activists or terrorists.

One such landing was on an island too small even to have a name. About 100 inhabitants lived in houses made of sugar canes and palm leaves built up on wooden stilts about 6ft off the ground. The most prominent of their buildings turned out to be 'The Glen Shop' where they sold cheap booze, and having finished our job that's where we all went.

The proprietor of the seedy-looking bar turned out to be a little white-haired old lady well into her 80s. Despite her deep tan it soon became obvious that she was as English as her name, and finding herself surrounded quite unexpectedly by a dozen or more Royal Marine Commandos she was thrilled to bits.

She asked our names and what towns we came from. Her name was Mrs Whitehouse. She had come over to Antigua with her husband 30 years before and after his death she had set up shop on the island. She asked me where I came from and when I said St Albans her face burst

into a huge smile. 'What a coincidence,' she said. 'St Albans is my home town too!' And when I started mentioning various members of the family it soon became obvious that she knew more about them than I did.

Mrs Whitehouse was my aunt. Our families had lost touch completely. So after all those years of separation I found myself on one of the remotest islands I'd ever seen, only to discover a relative I never even knew I had.

Nor did the coincidence end there. Two weeks later our ship called at Hamilton, the capital of Bermuda, and I went ashore on a shopping spree. The very first shop I walked into was a perfumier's and there behind the counter was a young lady who two years previously had worked as an assistant in my father's grocery shop.

Now one that happened in Capetown:

The Ferndale Male Voice Choir from Britain was on tour in South Africa giving concerts with the South African Navy Band. On the first night at the Arts Theatre, Capetown, a member of the choir thought he recognized a member of the band. On the second night the bandsman confirmed it, furthermore he reminded him where they last met. He showed him a programme for a production of *Cinderella* given in a POW Camp in Germany in 1945 in which they had 'starred' together.

In the audience that night was a man who recognized them both. He was the German warden in charge of their section of the POW camp.

Mrs Elizabeth Ibison, aged 86, was in Sharoe Green Hospital, Preston, Lancashire and she thought there was something familiar about the woman in the bed next to her. There was – but it was a week before she recognized Mrs Margaret Yates, aged 87, as her sister! They hadn't seen each other for 40 years.

They then started wondering what had

happened to their other sister, Mary, aged 84.

'She got married to a chap called Coulthurst,' said Margaret.

'Mary Coulthurst?' said the nurse. 'She's next door!'

And indeed she was in the neighbouring ward. So a stay in hospital turned in to a great family reunion.

And now, friends and lovers:

Whilst motoring south on our honeymoon in 1949, my husband and I remembered that we both had wartime friends living in the same county town on our route and decided to visit them.

We chose to call on my husband's colleague first, having got his address from the police station where he worked. Imagine my utter amazement when the door was opened by my nursing friend! They had married each other three weeks earlier.'

In a handbag?

We were on leave in London from overseas and my husband and I decided to have a few days in Paris. The night before we left, some friends gave us a party so we were feeling a little 'party-worn' to say the least when we arrived at the hotel after the journey. My husband had just enough strength (and change) to pay off the taxi from the Air Terminal before we collapsed in our room.

About half an hour later I pulled myself and my aching head together and decided to unpack – which is when I discovered to my horror I had no handbag.

Gone was all our money, sterling, francs and travellers cheques as I had insisted on holding the lot. 'But think woman! Where did you last have it?' In the taxi – so that's where I must have left it.

What could we do? In a hopeless gesture we plodded on foot back to the terminal in case the bag had been handed in – it hadn't. So with the few francs we had left we phoned the bank at home to stop the cheques.

We came out of the Terminal and walked about 100 yards down the road. The taxi driver and I recognized each other at the same moment! He turned a circle in the road, pulled up alongside us and produced my bag.

Now just imagine the chances of that happening out of all the taxis in Paris. Everything was intact, he again took us back to the hotel where he must have had the largest tip of his life!

Again we had a party that night!'

And sometimes it is a very bizarre world.

A few months ago I had a truly ghastly nightmare. I dreamt I was in an hotel in Bloomsbury – odd in itself as I never go to London if I can help it and have never been to Bloomsbury in my life. The hotel caught fire and I was trapped in my bedroom, unable to get out because the heat had warped the door-handle. I went through a traumatic hell waiting for help – there was nothing to do but wait and listen to the roaring of the flames (I have never been in or watched a big fire).

As with all nightmares, I finally wrenched myself awake, and in an effort to pull myself back to normality I switched on the bedside radio. This is what I heard: 'This is the 6 o'clock news. A serious fire broke out in the early hours of the morning at a hotel in Bloomsbury. One woman was burned to death and several other people were taken to hospital....'

Coincidence? It must have been, and yet.... As I said before, 'Nature caught in the act of rhyming.'

Operation Halley's Comet

A US Colonel issued the following directive to his Executive Officer: 'Tomorrow evening at approximately 20.00 hours Halley's Comet will be visible in this area, an event which occurs only once every 75 years. Have the men fall out in the battalion area in fatigues, and I will explain this rare phenomenon to them. In case of rain, we will not be able to see anything, so assemble the men in the theater and I will show films of it.'

Executive Officer to Company Commander: 'By order of the Colonel, tomorrow at 20.00 hours, Halley's Comet will appear above the battalion area. If it rains, fall the men out in fatigues; then march to the theater where the rare phenomenon will take place, something which occurs only once every 75 years.'

Company Commander to Lieutenant: 'By order of the Colonel in fatigues at 20.00 hours tomorrow evening, the phenomenal Halley's Comet will appear in the theater. In case of rain in the battalion area, the Colonel will give another order, something which occurs once every 75 years.'

Lieutenant to Sergeant: 'Tomorrow at 20.00 hours, the Colonel will appear in the theater with Halley's Comet, something which happens every 75 years. If it rains, the Colonel will order the comet into the battalion area.'

Sergeant to Squad: 'When it rains tomorrow at 20.00 hours the phenomenal 75-year-old General Halley, accompanied by the Colonel, will drive his Comet through the battalion area theater in his fatigues.'

STAGGERING FACTS

Both Presidents Lincoln and Kennedy were concerned with Civil Rights.
Lincoln was elected in 1860.
Kennedy was elected in 1960.
Both their wives lost children through death while in the White House.
Both men were killed on a Friday.
Both men were killed in the presence of their wives.
Both were shot in the head.
Both had successors named Johnson.
Both successors were Southern Democrats and both in the Senate.
Lincoln's successor, named Andrew Johnson, was born in 1808.
Kennedy's successor, named Lyndon Johnson, was born in 1908.
Booth, Lincoln's killer, was born in 1839.
Oswald, Kennedy's killer, was born in 1939.
Both assassins were Southerners favouring unpopular ideas.
Both were themselves assassinated before their trials.
Lincoln's secretary was named Kennedy.
Kennedy's secretary was named Lincoln.
Secretary Lincoln advised Kennedy not to go to Dallas.
Secretary Kennedy advised Lincoln not to go to the theatre.
Booth shot Lincoln in a theatre and ran to a warehouse.
Oswald shot Kennedy from a warehouse and ran to a theatre.

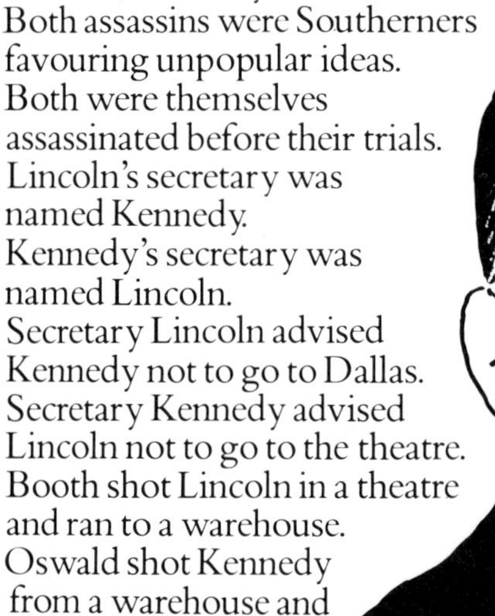

PALINDROMES

Those who enjoy playing with words can never resist a challenge. Palindromes (sentences that read the same backwards as forwards) were at their most popular in the last century, although the first one to appear in the English language did so a couple of hundred years before that:

LEWD DID I LIVE AND EVIL I DID DWEL

(No, he couldn't spell either!) That was followed not long after by one of the most famous – probably suggested by the capture of Napoleon:

ABLE WAS I ERE I SAW ELBA

And we were off!

A MAN, A PLAN, A CANAL - PANAMA

SUMS ARE NOT SET AS A TEST ON ERASMUS

I MAN AM REGAL! A GERMAN AM I

Probably the neatest I had sent to me was:

RISE TO VOTE, SIR

Chapter 11

Conversation Stoppers

Talking on the radio is like underwater wrestling – everything happens in slow motion. I am meant to be having a conversation with the listeners, but the reply (if there is one) comes through the post, by which time I've forgotten what I said. Under such circumstances you would hardly think listeners would send in conversation stoppers… you'd be wrong.

DID YOU KNOW that freeze-dried mashed potato isn't a recent invention. In the time of the Incas, the Indians of the Andes were the first producers of powdered mashed potato. They would lay out their potatoes, which froze overnight and went mushy the following day as they thawed out. In the morning the Indians would trample the mush and squeeze the water out. Repeating the process every day for a week they would produce a dried pulp which could be stored against hungry times.

DID YOU KNOW that just after his election as US President in 1912, Woodrow Wilson visited an aunt who was almost deaf. She asked him what kind of job he had and he bellowed into her ear-trumpet that he was now President.
'Of what?' inquired the old lady.
'Of the USA,' Wilson shouted back.
The aunt ended the discussion with a snort:
'Don't be silly, Woodrow!' she said.

DID YOU KNOW that the Post Office radio station at Slip End, Herts, now closed, once had to listen for a reply to a telegram transmitted to the Moon from Rugby, to please an eccentric customer. No, I didn't know that either.

DID YOU KNOW that a company in Tokyo that makes toilet rolls has started printing English lessons on them. It says anyone can expect to tear off eight hundred words in the first year of the course.

DID YOU KNOW that the idea of a bowler hat began more than a hundred years ago. A huntsman in Norfolk, William Coke by name, got fed up losing his tall hat every time he went over a fence, or when it was knocked off by an overhanging branch. In 1850 he went to a well-known hatter, William Beaulieu, and asked him to design him a new hunting hat. Beaulieu came up with the idea of a round hard felt hat, with a low crown. Coke could ride under low branches without losing the hat, and if he did fall off his horse the new hat acted as a sort of crash helmet. They called the hat the Beaulieu, then the bowler, which was easier to say.

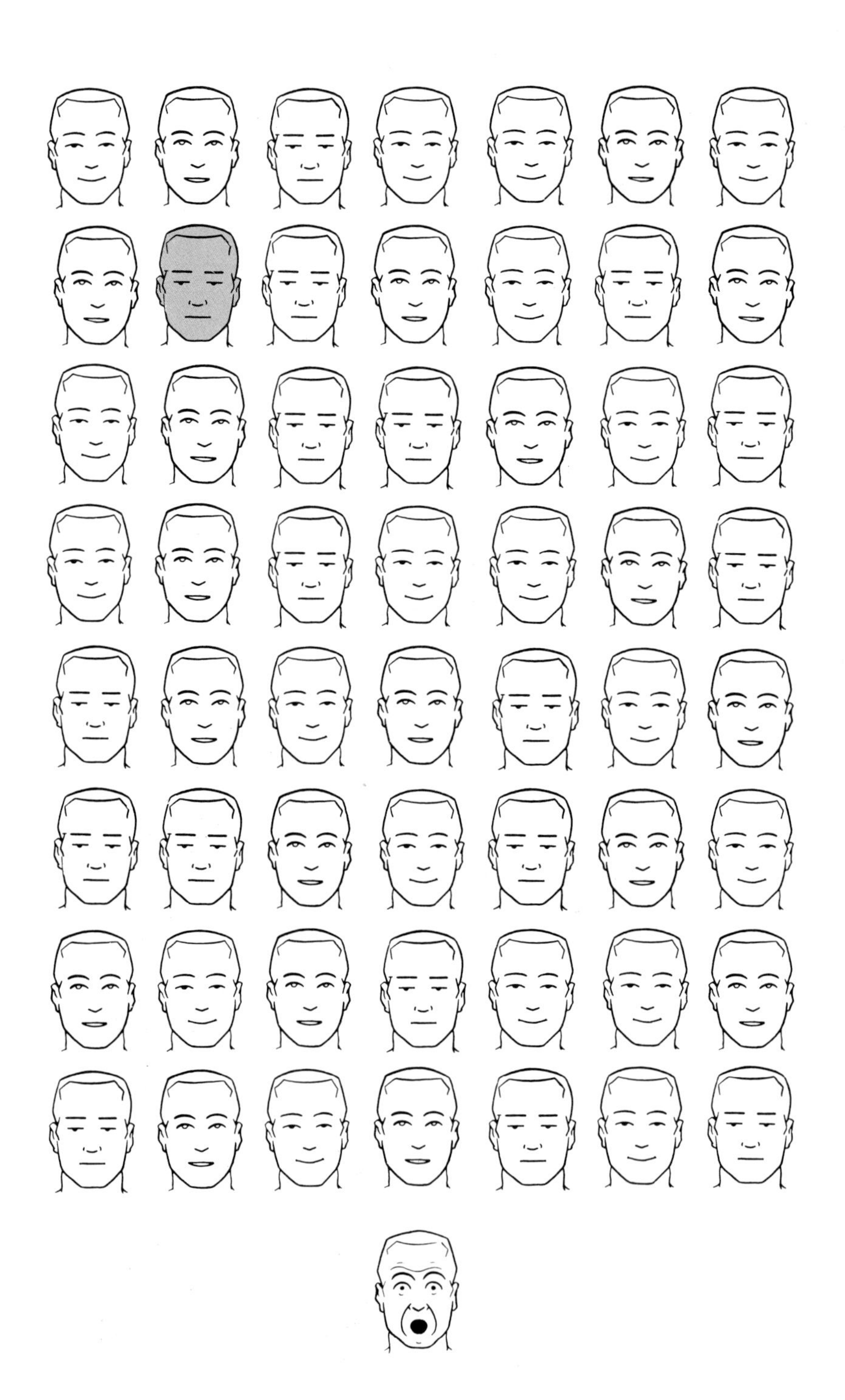

DID YOU KNOW that in World War II certain promising soldiers were sent on engineering courses. Special centres were set up all over the country for this purpose. The first postings were made alphabetically, in true military tradition. The result? Out of 300 soldiers arriving for one course, 298 were named Brown. Can you imagine the chaos on the command: 'Brown! Get fell in!'

DID YOU KNOW that it was once a capital offence to deface Westminster Bridge and also to impersonate a Chelsea pensioner? Also that:

In Connecticut it is illegal to ride a bicycle at more than 65 mph, carry corpses in a taxi or walk backwards after sunset.

In Hollywood it is illegal to drive more than two thousand sheep down Hollywood Boulevard at any one time.

There is a law prohibiting men from stealing after dark in Washington.

In Ohio it is illegal to borrow water, and men with hairy chests must wear shirts on the beach.

In Utah ladies' heels must not be more than 1½ in high.

In Virginia there is a law prohibiting ladies from attending a dance without wearing a corset.

In Alabama one may not wash one's hands in a public fountain, nor may one trade mules or live chickens after dark.

Chapter 12

Property Column

If you buy a house and live in it for a few years, by the time you go househunting again you will probably have forgotten that Estate Agents' English is not entirely the same language as the rest of us speak. So, next time you go viewing, be sure to have this glossary on your person.

Unusual elevation	Subsidence has started recently
Unusually designed	Subsidence started during building
An older type of property	Mortgage will be hard to get
A pre-war property	Mortgage will be impossible to get
A charming period property	No services
Small garden to front	A window box
Petite kitchen	A converted cupboard
Useful-sized garden	Minute
Gracious dwelling	Old
Scope for development	Unless you gut it, you can't live in it
Usual services	No gas, no electricity, no telephone
Ranch-type kitchen	Typist's misspelling of 'Range'
Architect-designed	The client's grandfather fancied himself

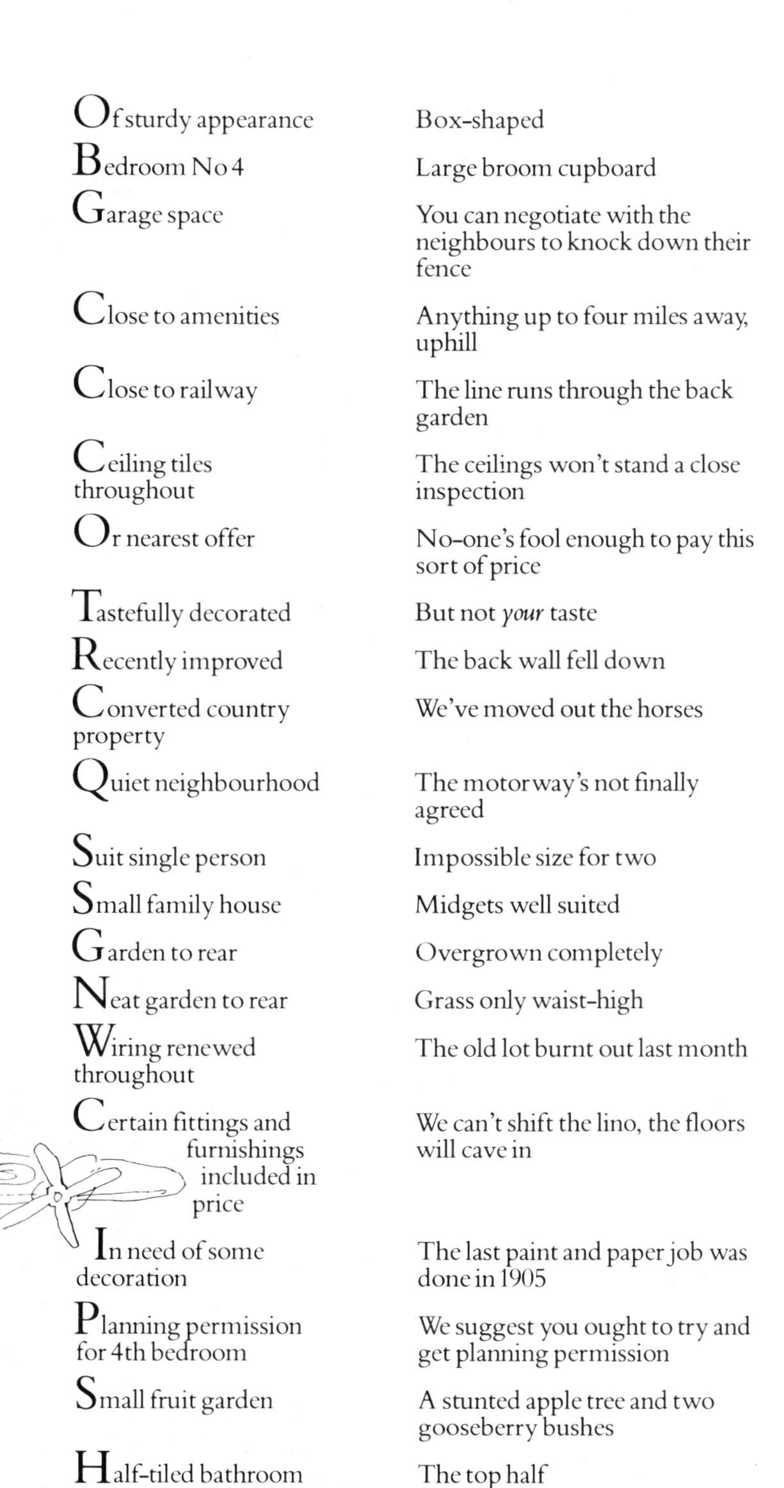

Of sturdy appearance	Box-shaped
Bedroom No 4	Large broom cupboard
Garage space	You can negotiate with the neighbours to knock down their fence
Close to amenities	Anything up to four miles away, uphill
Close to railway	The line runs through the back garden
Ceiling tiles throughout	The ceilings won't stand a close inspection
Or nearest offer	No-one's fool enough to pay this sort of price
Tastefully decorated	But not *your* taste
Recently improved	The back wall fell down
Converted country property	We've moved out the horses
Quiet neighbourhood	The motorway's not finally agreed
Suit single person	Impossible size for two
Small family house	Midgets well suited
Garden to rear	Overgrown completely
Neat garden to rear	Grass only waist-high
Wiring renewed throughout	The old lot burnt out last month
Certain fittings and furnishings included in price	We can't shift the lino, the floors will cave in
In need of some decoration	The last paint and paper job was done in 1905
Planning permission for 4th bedroom	We suggest you ought to try and get planning permission
Small fruit garden	A stunted apple tree and two gooseberry bushes
Half-tiled bathroom	The top half

Part-central heating	Heated towel-rail
Price now reduced	Surely *someone* wants this place
Peaceful area	Overlooking the cemetery
Recently come into our hands	Everyone else tried first
Unconventional appearance	The builder tried hard to get the walls straight
Compact kitchen	The size of a compact
Built-in cupboards	The previous owner thought he was a DIY expert
Late owner was ex-Army	The walls are full of bullet holes

We also heard about some good house names – and about some suitable occupants:

A New Zealand Air Force official by the name of Graves moved to an RAF Camp near Market Drayton. He bought a house in Cemetery Road and felt obliged to call it 'Tombstone View.'

A couple retired from India and called their house 'Pundrah' – very oriental! No, it's 'Hard-up' spelt backwards.

A Mr Inkpen of Hextable, Kent calls his house 'The Blots.'

On the way to Guildford is a bungalow called 'The Rasher' – presumably because it's on the Hog's Back.

A house overlooking the London-Crewe railway line is called 'Choo Choo View.'

They asked him what he'd named his house
'Tis Rusholme,' he replied.
But after he'd been wed a year
He called it Ellinside.

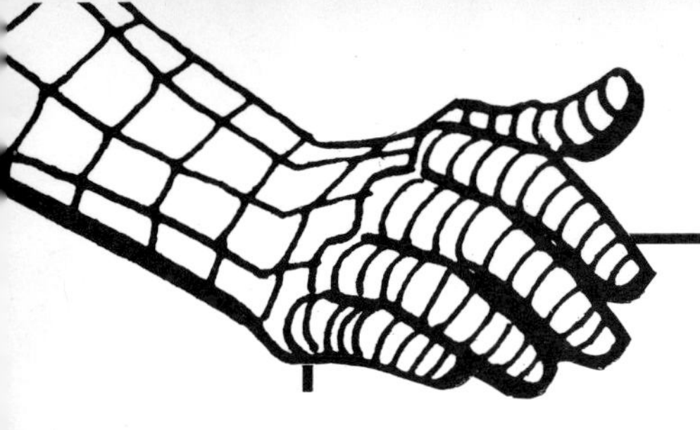

Chapter 13

Body Talk

In the words of Professor David L Thompson:

> Our language is full of suggestions that it is a privilege to work sitting down. We respect our chairman; we honour the throne; we speak of a professor's chair, a seat in parliament. The lawyer looks to the judge's bench; and the Turks speak of their divan, and the Hebrews of the sanhedrin, all in the same sense. Even the word president means the man in the best seat. All this betokens a habit of mind, respecting the man who does his work sitting down.

After all, as has been said many times – that's where he shines. But the human being is an amazing invention. Take the brain:

> Despite current, universal obeisance to the electronic computer, the human brain is far superior. It is self-propelled. It can be mass-produced by relatively unskilled labour. And it is very economical, needing little more than the equivalent of a handful of peanuts a day.

But all those little bits of food add up:

> Did you know that by the time an average man has reached the age of 70 he has eaten 100 tons of food, 1250 times the weight of his body? And that within the span of 70 years he walks far enough to reach the Moon, sleeps 13 years and eats for 6 years.

Furthermore:

> Most people speak at an average rate of 140 words per minute. Each one of us talks for about sixty minutes a day on average and if you talk that amount over an entire year it works out at more than $2\frac{1}{2}$ years in your whole lifetime.

The human statistics are endless – well almost:

> If all the toothpaste used in Scotland, England, Ireland and Wales in just twelve months were placed in one continuous line it would extend for sixty thousand miles – or about two and a half times around the Equator!

And it is not just a tough life for us humans alone. According to this label on a jar of honey:

> Honeybees have gathered nectar from approximately 4,500,000 clusters of clover and travelled about 150,000 miles, or equal to six times round the world, to deliver this honey to you.

Nor must all the blame for the world's problems be laid at the door of *homo sapiens*. The US Environmental Protection Agency says that the world's biggest source of air pollution is not the motor-car, it's not the aeroplane, the factory or even the cigarette:

> Burping cows must rank as the No 1 source of air pollution in the country. Cows burp 50 million tons of hydrocarbons into the atmosphere annually and 10 cows burp enough gas each year to provide heat, hot water and cooking gas requirements for a small home.

It's all very well to say that, why don't they *do* something? We have a world fuel problem! But in the long march of Everyman, what have we really achieved? Well, we're probably a little cleaner.

> Did you know that at the beginning of the 19th century the taking of a bath was looked upon as an event. Indeed, you were often looked upon as a crank if you took one. In the time of Lord Nelson not a single house in London had a proper bathroom. Windsor Castle didn't get one until the time of Edward VII and there was no bathroom in No 10 Downing Street until 1908. (As Mark Twain remarked: 'Soap and Education are not as sudden as a massacre, but they are more deadly in the long run.')

Here is some advice from a Chambers Dictionary published in 1739 on what to do about toothache:

> In the first stage of pain many find it useful to raise a blister behind each ear with a small cauterizing iron, but if the tooth be hollow and the pain persist, then cauterize the decayed tooth; some use a small iron nail heated to red heat, others prefer to plunge a red-hot scalpel into the offending part, and fill the hollow with mastic.

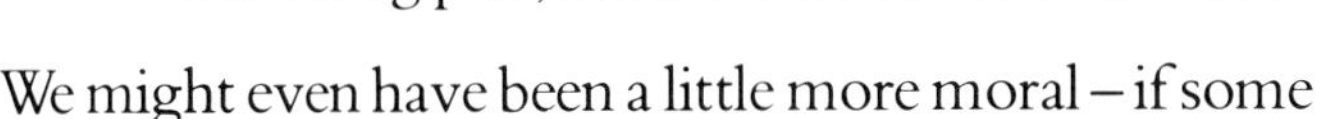

We might even have been a little more moral – if some had had their way. A book published in London in the year 1863 under the title *Etiquette* contained this advice:

> The perfect hostess will see to it that the works of male and female authors be properly separated on her bookshelves. Their proximity, unless they happen to be married, should not be tolerated.

And of course we know a lot more about ourselves, viz this extract from *Saxon's Book of Curious Facts:*

> It is a well known scientific fact that different people sound different vowels, when laughing; from which it is possible to draw the following conclusions: people who laugh in 'A' (ah) are frank, honest and fond of excitement, versatile but often of a fickle disposition. Laughter in 'E' (ay) is peculiar to phlegmatic and melancholy persons. Those who laugh in 'I' (EE) are children or simple-minded, obliging, affectionate, timid people of indecision. To laugh in 'O' indicates generosity and daring. Avoid if possible a person who laughs in 'U' as they are wholly devoid of principle.

In some things, however, we've only just arrived back at the beginning. Arabic numerals were designed by an unknown genius more than a thousand years ago, each digit being given a number of angles appropriate to its numerical value. So, starting with zero which has nil value, and therefore no angles, we have:

0123456789

Don't they look remarkably like the computer numbers printed at the bottom of our cheques? From which it is but a short leap to the highly suspect world of statistics, and this timely and patriotic warning:

IT'S TIME WE FACED UP TO YOUR RESPONSIBILITIES

or why it's your fault this country is on the rocks.

Population of the UK	50,124,680
People of 65 years or over	13,019,426
Balance left to do the work	37,105,254
People under 18	16,163,942
Balance left to do the work	20,941,312
People working for the government	10,628,143
Balance left to do the work	10,313,169
People in the armed forces	2,503,147
Balance left to do the work	7,810,022
People in the nationalised industries	7,608,629
Balance left to do the work	201,393
People in hospitals and asylums	132,420
Balance left to do the work	68,973
Spivs and those who don't work	56,973
Balance left to do the work	12,000
People in gaol	11,998
Balance left to do the work	2

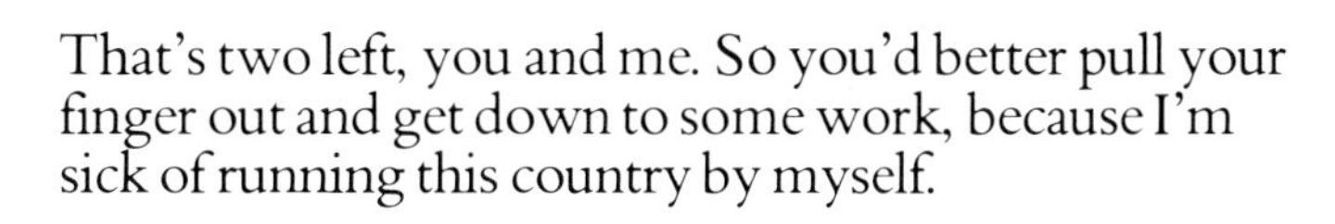
That's two left, you and me. So you'd better pull your finger out and get down to some work, because I'm sick of running this country by myself.

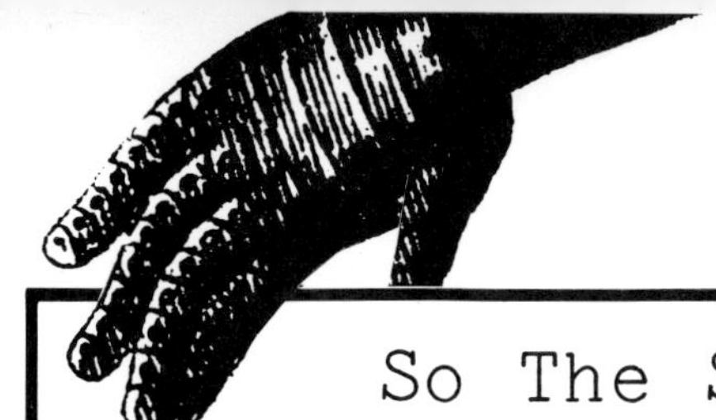

Chapter 14

So The Story Goes

Alfred Hitchcock once received a letter from a mother ambitious for her daugher. It read: 'I have a perfectly beautiful daughter. She is 17 years old, five feet three inches tall, blonde, and weighs eight stone. Do you think she might succeed in films?' Hitchcock replied: 'Madam, it would be impossible to say, as you did not state her width.'

Picasso wanted a wardrobe made in mahogany. He went to a local cabinetmaker, and to make his wishes clear he grabbed a piece of paper and sketched how he wanted the finished piece of furniture to look. 'How much will it be?' Picasso asked. 'Nothing,' replied the cabinetmaker. 'Just sign the sketch.'

Mark Twain attended an opera at which his hostess talked so much that no-one in her party was unable to enjoy the singing. Afterwards she asked Twain to be her guest a few days later. 'They are giving *Tosca* then,' she said. 'Charmed,' replied Twain, 'I've never heard you in that.'

Bishop Jacques Bossuet, the French theologist, once met a supercilious nobleman who remarked: 'I never go to church, as I've no doubt you've noticed. There are far too many hypocrites in churches.' 'Agreed,' replied the bishop, 'but you shouldn't let that stop you coming. We've always room for one more.'

The GP saw an elderly man stumble and fall in the busy main street and went over to help. As he bent over the man he was tapped on the shoulder and a voice said: 'Leave this to me. I'm a qualified first-aider.' The GP stepped aside and watched for a few minutes. Then he nudged the first-aider and confided: 'When you get to the bit when you send for the doctor, I'm here.'

Sir Noel Coward was asked by a television interviewer: 'Underneath everything, aren't you a man of granite?' 'Not in the least,' replied Coward. 'I'm a chocolate milk-shake with just a little vodka at the bottom.'

Close to the fourteenth hole on a golf course at Tarzana, California, there was a big drop into a treacherous, heavily wooded, marshy area and, of course, my ball rolled down there. When I started to go after it, my caddy said, 'Take a club.' 'How do I know what club to take? I can't see what the lie is.' 'It doesn't matter,' the caddy replied. 'It's for the snakes.' (Buddy Jackett in *The Truth about Golf and Other Lies*)

Marlene Dietrich once gave a portrait sitting to one of Hollywood's top photographers. When the proofs were shown to her she was unimpressed. 'No,' she said, 'I don't like them – any of them. Last time I sat for you, six years ago, the pictures were magnificent. But now...' The photographer smiled and said: 'Ah, yes, Miss Dietrich. But you must remember I was six years younger then.'

When violinist Jascha Heifetz made his now-legendary début at Carnegie Hall (he was 13) New York was taken by storm. Many famous musicians were present including Mischa Elman the violinist, and pianist Moriz Rosenthal. About half an hour into the recital Elman turned to Rosenthal and said: 'My God. It's hot in here!' 'Not for pianists,' replied Rosenthal.

Once during the Sixties Jack Warner of Warner Brothers returned to America from Europe to be told that one of his greatest actors, Ronald Reagan, was to run for Governor of California. His reply was: 'No, no, no! Jimmy Stewart for Governor. Reagan for his best friend.'

Alan Jay Lerner of *My Fair Lady* fame took two weeks to write the last lines of Eliza's song *Wouldn't It Be Lovely*. He eventually came up with 'Luverly, Luverly, Luverly, Luverly.'

Cherubini was for many years the Director of the Conservatoire in Paris. On one occasion he listened patiently to a very persistent singer. 'You have a big voice,' he finally said. The singer was delighted. 'Yes, a very big voice. Why don't you become an auctioneer?'

The composer Handel was rehearsing his opera *Flavio* when he had a row with an English singer called Gordon. 'You are not following me.' The young man replied: 'If you don't look out, I'll jump down off the stage onto your harpsichord and smash it to pieces!' 'You do that,' said Handel. 'Just let me know when and I'll sell tickets. More people will come to see you jump than will come to hear you sing!'

The first time Elizabeth Taylor was kissed by Richard Burton she burped. They were filming *Cleopatra* and the scene had to be reshot.

WC Fields once made his living by 'drowning.' He would go in for a swim and fake an emergency so he had to be rescued by the Life Guards. As he was being 'revived' the lemonade and hot dog stands did great business and Fields got a cut from the profits.

Albert Einstein was once asked how it was that man had been clever enough to split the atom but not clever enough to avoid making a weapon of mass destruction from it. 'Because,' he said, 'physics is less complicated than politics.'

Mrs Eleanor Roosevelt is reported to have remarked that although she was flattered to have a rose named after her, she was not so pleased to read in the catalogue: 'Mrs Eleanor Roosevelt: no good in a bed, but fine up against a wall.'

HEY! LOOK SOMEBODY'S DROWNING. LET'S HAVE A HOTDOG
HOT DOGS

Chapter 15

Beer Sale! Kew Earley!

For me the Place Name Game started on journeys back to school after the holidays, when I realized that the last four stations had the makings of a gory tale: 'Why kill 'em – cart 'em to Canterbury' (Wye, Chilham, Chartham, Canterbury). But its full flowering came with the motoring reports that in the winter months used to clog up our programmes, particularly in the early mornings. There were no rules. You simply had to make up sentences using as many place names and as few other words as possible. Some were short and pithy:

Eye Havant Nocton Diss Dore!

Wye Ware Cardigan Over Churt? Chile?

Others were more leisurely:

The Road Leeds Uphill Over Wild Open
Rough Common Nomansland. Lower Down
Andover Crossroads, Halfway Towards The
Priory, Inoa Hundred Acres Ware Eye Cann
Brede Jersey Cowes Ore Mabie Lye Neath Oaks
Orby The Green River Bank.
Whyle Eyam Hardley Prosperous, Iver
Stonehouse Bacup The Moor, Wyche, Inverie
High Easter Leigh Windsor Coldrain Wilby
Well Worth Owning.

Try some more:

Rose Ash Rushton Loose Girdle Fell Six Mile
Bottom Oldham Orsett Downe.

Askham Wye Ugley Harold Wood March
Severn Matching Cowes West Down Street
Andover Bridge Forres Freshwater Bath.

Tooting Atherstone Wall, Virginia Water
Preston, Forfar Over Valley Andover
Ironbridge Maryland Nelson Ware Hitchin
Ryde Northwood.

Stepaside! Wye? Cowes.

Puddletown – Ware? Isle of Dogs? Scilly!

Occasionally we were even given advice (some people
just can't resist it):

What to do with an old pair of trousers?
Patcham, Lyneham, Wareham.

Some went further than mere advice:

> Our Father who art in Hendon, Holloway be thy Staines, thy Kingston come, thy Wimbledon in Erith as it is in Heston. Give us Foots Cray our daily Brent and forgive us our West Ham as we forgive them that Westminster against us. Lead us not into Thames Station but deliver us from Esher, for thine is the Kenton, the Purley and the Hooley, for Enfield and Edgware. Gravesend.

And some of the stories were quite touching:

> Chalmleigh Stanley Gailey Leeds Maiden Bradley Gretna Green.
> 'Eye Havant Pill,' Mumbles Bride.
> Stanley, Wittering Over Beer: 'Rest and Be Thankful.'

And through it all we had what were called Songs for Swinging Road-hogs – and they arrived in their thousands:

> Highgate a Kick Out of Looe.
> Burton up your overcoat.
> The Bury thought of you.
> Keep Brighton to the end of the road.
> You're the Cheam in my coffee.
> On a Slough boat to China.
> My heart Strood still.
> Thame on my hands.
> Ticket to Ryde.
> Yarmouth have been a beautiful baby!
> Peebles, who need Peebles.
> Let's Calderhall thing off.
> If I were Harwich man.
> God be in Minehead and in my understanding.
> Hythe got you under my skin.
> Cannock canoe you down the river.
> Chathamnooga Choo-Choo.
> Stoke gets in my eyes.
> Some enchanted evening, Yeovil see a stranger.
> Sunbury loves me; I wonder who.
> Highgate too hungry for dinner at eight.
> If I had a Torquay Picture of You.

For Esher Jolly Good Fellow.
Wembley Red, Red Robin Comes
Bob-bob-bobbin' along.
Harrow, Harrow, Who's Your Lady Friend.
Seaton On the Dock of the Bay.
Diss Nearly Was Mine.
Boom Bangor Bang.

Inevitably, before long we were on to football teams:

The marriage of Montague and Gill Ingham (born Mouth) was Brechin up. No longer were their Hearts United. With most marriages, if the husbands are Rovers it Wrexham. And so it was with Montague and Gill. All she wanted to do was stay at home Reading books, while he had a yearning Forfar off places like the Orient. He said: 'A Man's field of endeavour must be where ambition Leeds him.' So, with that, Mont rose from his chair and, leaving his front Torquay on the mantelpiece, left to join the navy.

He went to a South port where he joined the Crewe of a ship. They set sail on Wednesday for a New Port which lay across the Swan Sea. Montague's job was to Stoke the boilers and he spent the voyage Working ton upon ton of coal into the furnace. This ensured that the fire was a Brighton and that they could steam at a rate of Notts. At the end of the voyage there was just one Morton of coal left. So, when they anchored in the Clyde, Montague went ashore to buy some more. The coal merchant didn't know Montague, so he said: 'What for d'ye want the Black burning stuff?'

When Montague told him the merchant lent him a Barrow to take the coal back to the ship. As Montague had no money with him he had to get the coal on credit or, as they say in France, par tick!

Meanwhile, back at the ship, a Link on one of the anchor chains broke. As it takes two anchors to Oldham the ship drifted onto the Clydesbank and damaged its Hull. The shock was almost enough to kill Marnock the captain. There was his ship with its bows Pressed on to the South end of the Port's mouth, so he had to pay off his men.

Montague by this time felt he had been Away long enough. The Draw of Home was too much for him.

Now he and Gill Ayr United once again, and their Cup Finally runneth over.

Somehow, Hearts were always in the writers' Arsenal:

Dear John Dunn,
I've been Tottenham up and I make it thirty-six names. I think that's a Stirling effort, don't you? I'm Bolton down to the pillar box now to catch the post, but I'll Walsall the way home again. Please excuse the letter: I would have put it on a Cardiff it had been shorter but it was Chester bit too long. I won't sign my name Leicester suspicious boss asks me what I've Dundee safternoon.

Brentford saw Aberdeen in Queens Park. He said Alloa is your Motherwell? She replied no we had to Bury her last Wednesday. He said my Hearts for you, marry me and I'm sure you'll have Leicester worry about. She said are you one of those Wolves who Leeds a girl into a Forest and afterwards sends her to Coventry? If you agree to get up Brighton early, Stoke the fire, hoover the Chesterfield, polish the Rangers, and when you've Dundee housework take me out in the Carlisle marry you. Oh and two more things, I like a drink, so don't forget to Stockport and lemon, and when you bring home your wages on a Friday, I'll Oldham.

Guard Dogs Operating

'Words, words, words. I'm so sick of words,' sang Eliza Doolittle, wailing against the teachings of Professor Higgins. And I'm sure we can all sympathize. The trouble with words is they so easily get out of control – like a wet whippet they slip from your grasp and speed off on their own. There was, for example, a doctor in Leicester who was talking about the organization of his group practice to an audience of school parents, and he said:

> The good thing about Health Centres is that whereas one doctor does not generate enough work for a midwife, a number of doctors in a Health Centre do....

Now, do you suppose he really meant what we thought he said? On the other hand, an international medical magazine probably did mean:

> The family planning problem is frequently so badly presented that it is improperly understood and sometimes gives rise to absurd misconceptions.

– or something like it. All too often it's the search for brevity that causes the problem. From Harrogate came this sign:

> White Hart Hospital – Guard Dogs Operating

Clever things. Then this, from a Births column:

> **ELLIS** To Liz and Bob on June 23rd – twin daughters. By cable from New Zealand.

And this, from the classified ads:

> Hire a self-drive car from the Station Garage for your holiday, wedding or funeral.

But for complete economy of words, this would be hard to beat:

It is however possible to go too far and become miserly with words:

> A major company with international branches recently realized that the word 'Regards' when routinely added to all outgoing cables was costing the company about £400 a year. A memo was sent to all offices: 'In future, please end all cables with no regards.' For several weeks thereafter 'No regards' began appearing at the end of all outgoing cables, increasing cable costs even more and adding nothing to friendly relations.

And speaking of friendly relations, here's a quote from Judge Lyons at Liverpool Crown Court, reported in the *Liverpool Echo*:

> Putting the boot in and kicking people in the face must be stamped out in South Lancashire.

Which leads us on to the use of slang – the casual phrase that you might get away with in conversation but not in print:

> The flight you mention is completely booked, but we will inform you immediately someone drops out, which usually happens.

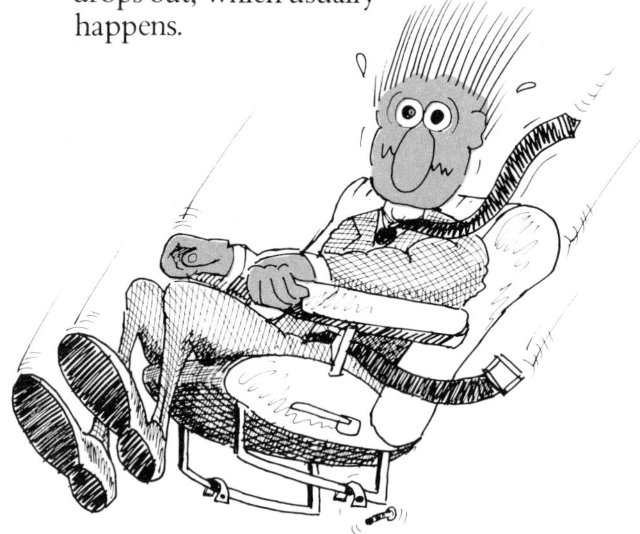

> CRASH COURSES available for those wishing to learn to drive very quickly – Abbey SOM Phone 20860.

The Parish Magazine is a good source:

> The preachers for the following six weeks are nailed up in the porch.

> The old churchyard has been sadly neglected because there have been no burials there for over 30 years. An appeal is to be launched to encourage voluntary bodies to remedy the situation.

And there is sometimes a feeling that a Divine (or otherwise) hand has been at work. At Christmas a few years ago a Bristol church used the technique of stick-on letters to shout its message:

GLORY TO GOD IN THE HIGHEST

Alas, there is always one letter that doesn't stick properly. Why did it have to be the last 'E':

GLORY TO GOD IN THE HIGH ST

Then there was the cheery motoring journalist who wrote:

> The use of a conventionally sloping rear window enables parcels to be carried on the shelf beneath and there is ample room for passenger's heads, should they wish to drop off during a journey.

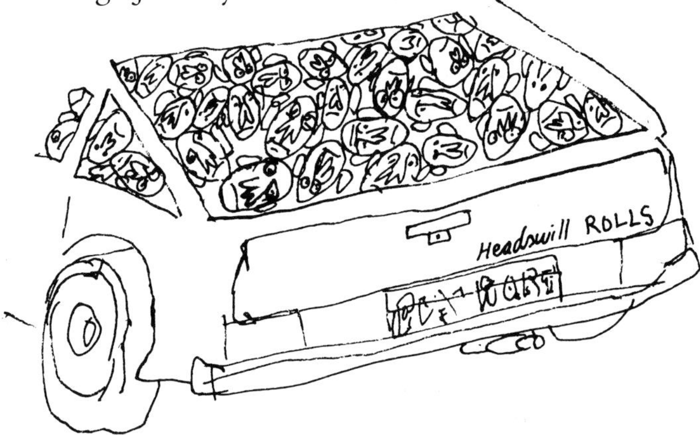

And what should the headless passenger wear? 'Air Wear Everywhere' was a handy guide put out some years ago by BOAC. Under 'Bombay' you read:

> Between March and November only the lightest clothes are needed. Take enough washable outfits to allow several changes a day. Evening dress is very rarely worn, and women need only wear stockings for cocktail parties.

But we can't always blame the journalists. All too often they are merely reporting what they were told. Victor Wilson of Eye, Northants, for instance, was run over while working on his car by his young son who managed to get it into gear. Arriving at the hospital with an injured leg he was quoted as saying:

> I was hopping mad at first, but Shaun is simply car mad.

This one is worth reprinting in full:

> **IRISHMAN WAS NUDE IN TREE**
>
> An Irish medical student who was found up a tree stark naked was fined £30 at Witham

Magistrates' Court on Monday for assault on a police officer.

Roy Murphy, 20, of no fixed address, pleaded guilty to the charge. An officer told the court that on Sunday night PC Peter Frost saw somebody lurking in a garden in Goldhanger. When he approached, the man made off but PC Frost tracked him to the foot of a tree. At the bottom of the tree was a pile of clothes and at the top was Murphy – stark naked.

PC Frost called to him to come down and at first he refused. Then he jumped down and attempted to run off.

He was caught by the officer and a 'fair struggle' ensued, in which PC Frost was grabbed between the legs.

In court, Murphy, a student at Dublin University, working at Goldhanger Fruit Farm during his vacation, said he was very sorry. He could not remember anything about the incident. He had had too much to drink. Passing sentence, Mr Alfred Playle, chairman of the bench, told him he must not take the law into his own hands.

So, the newspapers set out in print either what we say or, in the advertisements, what their customers ask them to say. These two should get together:

GENT 35, interested in starting stud livery yard, seeks lady partner with some experience. Genuine replies only – Box PFT 2.

MARRIED MAN required urgently for PRIVATE STUD. Good 3-bedroomed house. One mile from village and school. Only those with first-class references need apply.

Or, for fish fanciers:

ST BRELADE'S AQUARIA now open. Red House, St Brelade (next to fish and chip shop). Specialist selection of Tropical and Goldfish.

And after the fish and chips – the bangers!

TRAINEE cannon ball required for test firing of new cannon, must be able to withstand shock and prepared to travel. Ring 4124, evenings 2218.

No mention of the calibre of potential applicants. But talking of explosions, occasionally one gets a hint of the pent-up frustration and anger against authority that lies behind some ads:

HOLE IN THE ROAD FOR SALE Outside the Queens Arms public-hostelry at Victoria, London SW1. COMPLETE with red lamps and barrier, and mud from excavation; ALMOST NEW hole; only September last; must be GOING CHEAP: no one interested in it: Offers to the Chief Engineer, County Hall, Westminster, or the Chief Engineer, London Electricity Board. Tours of the excavation can be arranged by the frustrated Lady licensee and her neighbours.

LOOK WHAT I'VE JUST BOUGHT

And I would love to know more about this:

THANKS

CHIVERTON Mrs Chiverton wishes to thank the kind gentleman for all his help and understanding in her hour of need on the night of August 27th.

All in all, ours is a confusing language – which is why foreigners say we make good diplomats but bad marriage partners. But at least the foreigners try and speak it, even if their efforts don't always come out quite right. A notice for British tourists in a Greek hotel read:

We are pleased to invite you for our Scandinavian Buffet in our Taverna to-night. This is also our occasion to wear your suites and dresses.

And from a travel brochure:

> Enjoy our large, airy rooms, home-type food, diets catered to. Scandinavian pastry, home-made bread, country-fresh eggs. Hospital is the aim here.

And we haven't even started on the spelling of English! So, just in case any foreigners have picked up this book looking for enlightenment, perhaps we could end this section with a few tips:

HINTS ON PRONUNCIATION FOR FOREIGNERS

I take it you already know
Of 'tough' and 'bough' and 'cough' and 'dough'?
Others may stumble, but not you
On 'hiccough', 'thorough', 'laugh' and 'through'
Well done! And now you wish perhaps
To learn of less familiar traps.

Beware of 'heard', a dreadful word
That looks like 'beard' and sounds like 'bird'
And 'dead'. It's said like 'bed', not 'bead'
(for goodness sake don't call it 'deed'!)
Watch out for 'meat' and 'great' and 'threat'
They rhyme with 'suite' and 'straight' and 'debt'.

A 'moth' is not a moth in 'mother'
Nor 'both' in 'bother', 'broth' in 'brother'
And 'here' is not a match for 'there'
Nor 'dear' and 'fear' for 'bear' and 'pear'
And then there's 'dose' and 'nose' and 'lose'
Just look them up – and 'goose' and 'choose'.

And 'cork' and 'work' and 'card' and 'ward'
And 'font' and 'front' and 'ward' and 'sword'
And 'do' and 'go' and 'thwart' and 'cart'
Come come we've hardly made a start
A dreadful language? Man Alive
I'd mastered it when I was five!

PLURALS

We'll begin with a box and the plural is boxes,
But the plural of ox is oxen, not oxes,
Then one fowl is a goose, but two are called geese
Yet the plural of moose should never be meese.
You may find a lone mouse or a whole set of mice
Yet the plural of house is houses not hice
If the plural of man is always called men
Why shouldn't the plural of pan be called pen?
If I speak of a foot and you show me your feet
And I give you a boot, would a pair be called beet?
If one is a tooth and a whole set are teeth
Why should not the plural of booth be beeth?
Then one may be that and three would be those
Yet hat in the plural wouldn't be hose.
We speak of a brother and also of brethren
But though we say mother, we never say methren
Then the masculine pronouns are he, his and him
But imagine the feminine she, shis and shim!

INSURANCE CLAIMS
I
MARRIAGE ANNOUNCEMENTS
M
L
LETTERS TO THE TAX INSPECTOR
INSURANCE CLAIMS
I
INSURANCE CLAIMS
I
MARRIAGE ANNOUNCEMENTS
M
L
INSURANCE CLAIMS
I
MARRIAGE ANNOUNCEMENTS
M
L
LETTERS TO THE TAX INSPECTOR
INSURANCE CLAIMS
I
L
INSURANCE CLAIMS
I
MARRIAGE ANNOUNCEMENTS
M
L